Praise for *THEM: The Richer Life*

John has beautifully illustrated ways to carry out the Great Commandment of loving one another. He looks at loving relationships in a fresh way, using clever chapter titles and a text illustrated by his own life to demonstrate multi-directional healing when good relationships happen. I am eager to own, read and share this good book!
~ Dr. Laura Mae Gardner, Wycliffe and SIL International Personnel Consultant

John Certalic has done a masterful job of weaving his own story with humor while revealing the deep insights he has learned on this journey. You will find yourself wanting to put the book down after each chapter so you can run out and find someone to love well!
~ Devri Wickwire, Missionary to Cyprus and Asia

The author's honesty, vulnerability and compassion in sharing his life story caused me to examine my own life story. It has made me ask the hard questions he raises in dealing with fear, anger, depression, and unforgiveness—all so that I can find God's healing and restoration. ~ Suzanne, former ESL teacher in China

Wow, what a wonderfully refreshing book. John's ability to weave his personal life stories into powerful principles is both heartwarming and challenging. This book is a great read for anyone who has any desire to improve their relationships with people.
~ Pat Petkau, Executive Director, Forest Springs Camp and Conference Center

If you believe, as I do, that the most important thing in life is our relationships, then THEM is the kind of book that can help in the most important area of life. I have learned much from John Certalic about relationships. So many have benefited from his wisdom in Greater Milwaukee and in many other places, and I, for one, am excited to see some of it now available in written form. THEM is deep and moving and wise, while full of needed humor, since the text leads us into the depths of our relational issues. Be ready for John's storytelling to cause reflection on your own life and relationships as the narrative and the wisdom here call us to move beyond inherent human self-centeredness toward loving relationships. And you just may have trouble putting it down, as I did.
~ Bill Oliverio, Ph.D., Pastor, Immanuel Church and Lecturer in Theology, Marquette University, Milwaukee, WI

In THEM, you'll be struck by John's authentic style of writing and relating. I personally lived chapter four of this book, where John graciously got into my sinking boat. I am still in the ministry today, forever indebted to his care for me...incarnating HIS care for me! I recommend this book for missionaries, pastors and their staff, Bible college and seminary faculty and students, small group leaders, and anyone who wants to live a richer relational journey by caring for others, or caring for just...THEM! ~ Mike Frans, Grace Church Pastor, Delafield, WI

THEM transforms a broad array of real life experiences into a rich understanding of the dynamics of our need for, and the effects of true caring. Readers will appreciate the smoothness of flow, the depth of perception, and the foundation and power of true redemption in caring.
~ John Powell, Ph.D., Professor Emeritus, Michigan State University, Co-Founder, Annual Conference on Mental Health and Missions

After serving nearly 13 years on the mission field and seeing many fellow missionaries go home due to member-care issues, I appreciate the effort and work that went into this book. By sharing his own personal journey and stories, John Certalic passes on to the reader his wisdom and insights into being a healthy child of God and caring for others. I highly recommend this book. ~ EG, missionary serving in Europe

THEM

The Richer Life Found in Caring for Others

THEM

The Richer Life Found in Caring for Others

John M. Certalic

As you care well for THEM, may it bring out the best that is YOU.

John M. Certalic

ROMANS 12:9-21

HenschelHAUS
publishing, inc.

Milwaukee, Wisconsin

Unless otherwise indicated, all Scripture quotations are taken from the Holy Bible, New Living Translation, copyright © 1996, 2004, 2007 by Tyndale House Foundation. Used by permission of Tyndale House Publishers, Inc., Carol Stream, Illinois 60188. All rights reserved.

Bible passages marked NIV refer to Scriptures taken from the HOLY BIBLE, NEW INTERNA-TIONAL VERSION ®. Copyright © 1973, 1978, 1984 by International Bible Society. Used by permission of Zondervan. All rights reserved.

The Four Spiritual Laws described in Chapter 7 are from *Have You Heard of the Four Spiritual Laws?* written by Bill Bright, © 1965-2016 The Bright Media Foundation and Campus Crusade for Christ, Inc. All rights reserved. http://crustore.org/four-spiritual-laws-outline/ Included by permission.

In some cases the names and identifying details of individuals described in this book have been changed to protect their privacy.

Published by
HenschelHAUS Publishing, Inc.
www.henschelHAUSbooks.com
Please contact the publisher for academic or non-profit discounts.

ISBN: 978159598-455-5
E-ISBN: 978159598-456-2
Library of Congress Control Number: 2016932396

Publisher's Cataloging-In-Publication Data
(Prepared by The Donohue Group, Inc.)
Names: Certalic, John M.
Title: THEM : the richer life found in caring for others / John M. Certalic.
Other Titles: Richer life found in caring for others
Description: Milwaukee, Wisconsin : HenschelHAUS Publishing, Inc., [2016]
Identifiers: LCCN 2016932396 | ISBN 978-1-59598-455-5 (print) |
    ISBN 978-1-59598-456-2 (ebook)
Subjects: LCSH: Certalic, John M. | Counselors--Biography. | Missionaries--Pastoral counseling
    of. | Caring--Anecdotes. | Helping behavior--Anecdotes.
Classification: LCC BV2094.6 .C47 2016 (print) | LCC BV2094.6 (ebook) | DDC 266.001/9--dc23

Cover design by Hope Certalic
Author photo by Nikki Allen

Printed in the United States of America

*To my wife, Janet, whom I've known since we first met
at age thirteen in her father's garage,
and who has been modeling for me ever since
the richness found in living a life of caring for others.*

Table of Contents

Foreword

John Certalic cares about people. And he cares deeply about people who don't care! Drawing deeply from his own life story which he tells with transparency, candor, wry humor and moving detail, plus his own studies in psychology, he explains why so often we don't care. To this he adds what he has learned from his wide experience as a counselor and friend to hurting people from many cultures.

As he explores the inner dynamics of the uncaring soul, he unearths surprises and challenges, and proposes spiritual, psychological and immensely practical remedies. As John tells of the discoveries he made himself as he learned to care, he reveals the blessings that accrue to the person who dares to care.

This is a rare book because it is easy to read, but it will make you uneasy, and then ease you into ways that will bring help and encouragement where greatly needed. You will be eased into solutions to deep-rooted issues that we may never have recognized. And you'll be eased into the joy of being blessed by the God who invented caring in the first place, and who has grieved that we humans are so frequently sparing in our caring.

—Stuart Briscoe, Pastor, Author, Broadcaster

Preface

Writers occasionally describe a book they started writing as one that began to take on a life of its own. They speak of how the path they intended to walk down took a detour, and they ended up following the path the book took them, rather than the other way around. This is one of those books.

When I began this project, I had in mind to write a book on how missionaries could better care for each other. You may not know any missionaries. You may even be like my former neighbor, Joe, who when he learned that my career is all about caring for missionaries, responded with, "I hate missionaries! What gives those people the right to try to change other people? They should just leave people alone!" Unlike my neighbor, I know many missionaries and find them to be some of the most interesting people in the world.

A book on helping missionaries better care for each other could, I thought, be a potential solution to a problem WEC International, a large mission agency, identified in a 1990s research study. They found that 5,400 North American missionaries leave the mission field every year for "preventable reasons." Maybe in some small way, I could help prevent the preventable by writing a how-to book to give missionaries ideas of how they could better relate to each other. For when missionaries leave the mission field prematurely, it's often because of relationship problems.

But as I got into the writing, and after showing early drafts to trusted readers, the comment kept coming back to me that the book would appeal to an audience broader than just the missionary community. They said what they were reading was just as applicable to non-missionaries. After all, most of us want better relationships. Whether missionary or not, we are relational beings who need each other.

Another path this book took me down was re-thinking my initial thought to write a how-to book about building better relationships by caring for others. There's certainly a place for how-to books, but the more I got into this effort, the more I realized what moved me to care better for people were stories of seeing it done well. If we are careful observers of the human condition, we'll find examples all around us of people caring for each other that will inspire us to do a better job of it ourselves.

As I was thinking this through, I remembered the time I fell asleep in my high school history class. I was up late the night before at my after-school job, and coupled with how boring history was taught at the time, I dozed off. This so irritated my teacher that he sent me to the office for my one and only behavior problem in four years. It's probably still on my permanent record. History was so dull then, so many facts and events to remember, like the Dred Scott Decision, the founding of Rhode Island in 1636, and the Teapot Dome Scandal. Who cares?

But later, when I was in college, also with a late-night part-time job, history came alive to me and sparked within me an interest in a whole new fascinating world. There were even more facts, but they became the frames around wonderful paintings of stories. Stories of great ideas, and great people who expanded my mind and gripped my heart. I learned how the more time passes, and the more things change, the more they remain the same.

I was privileged to have great history professors who excelled at telling stories that motivated me to understand what drives us, what motivates us to be people of heroic accomplishment, unspeakable evil, and everything in between. I took every class I could from my advisor,

Dr. Walter Wussow, because he was so good at telling stories that made history come alive. He spoke often of the years he spent in France doing research for his dissertation on the French Revolution. With great passion, he shared how chance encounters with a French farmer, or a clerk at the bakery, would reveal themes and a worldview shaped by a thousand years of French history. The stories are what mattered; they were the Mona Lisa. The names, dates, and events of history were only the frame to hold the painting together.

The painting, the story, I want this book to depict is how we can experience better relationships by caring better for each other. It's a life-giving story of getting by giving. Something so counterintuitive for the times in which we live, something difficult for us to appreciate.

Author Donald Miller describes the value of story this way, "If you want people to understand and identify with a complicated concept, tell a story about it. Telling a story often creates a 'clicking experience' in a person's brain, allowing them to suddenly understand what someone else is trying to say. As such, those who can tell good stories will create faster, stronger connections with others."

More than something that clicks in our brains, I hope the stories of caring for others in this book unlocks something in the heart of each reader.

So even if you're like my former neighbor Joe, who hates missionaries, may your heart be touched. Touched in ways to act that bring out the best in you as you experience the richness in relationships found in caring well for others. May these stories speak to you and inspire you as they have me.

January 2016

Chapter 1

People are Like Houses

The older I grow, the more I listen to people who don't talk much..
—Germain G. Glidden

There's a building in the South Carolina town where our daughter lives known as *All About Me*. The name on the building sticks out its chest, and with hands on hips, smiles at you as it declares in big bold letters: it's *All About Me*. It's the All About Me building, home to several small retail boutiques. I don't think you're allowed to buy a gift for someone else in these stores, because it is all about me. I hear they even have security guards on duty to prevent this kind of thing. The building is owned by the wife of the Baptist pastor in town.

There's a part of me that appreciates the brutal honesty of the building's name, a tribute to consumerism and self-interest. It says it like it is. No apologies for what it is. There's another part of me, however, that cringes inside. I wonder if the town's Baptist pastor cringes. Really, is it all about me? Sometimes it should be, like when we're infants and can't feed ourselves, and when we're in hospice, and … can't feed ourselves. Then it's appropriate to be all about me. But everywhere in between? I hope not.

The same uneasy feeling I have when I drive past *All About Me* is the same feeling I have in writing a book about caring for others. It puts me a bit on edge, because who am I to write about caring for others when I do such a poor job of it myself? When I take an honest look at how I live, more often than not, *it is* all about me, and so little about caring for others. Over the years, I have unwittingly become an expert in living a self-centered life. It comes so naturally to me. I don't have to practice it at all. But I am learning to move from an *all about me* life, to one with more meaning and fulfillment found in caring for others.

These are my credentials for writing a book on ways we can all better care for each other. They're the same kind of credentials a formerly-fat person has in writing a weight loss book. A recovering-fat person who still on occasion eats a box of Oreos with a banana split. Or the same qualifications as someone whose out-of-control spending sends that person into bankruptcy, but who eventually gets out of debt to live a financially responsible life—yet still, at times, will buy Calvin Klein underwear at Nordstrom rather than Fruit of the Loom at Walmart.

Imperfect people who learn from their mistakes inspire me. Perfect people who write books about what they do instinctively discourage me. You know the kind of books I'm talking about, the book about de-cluttering one's life by someone who's been a neat freak all her life. Or the book about how to remodel your bathroom by the guy who was born with a tape measure in one hand and a hammer in the other. This book is so not like that.

What I've written is born from mistakes I've made and all that is wrong with me in caring mostly about myself. You will read what I am learning in following hard after God, and trying to reflect His image well. Nothing within these pages is about some innate inherited skill or temperament of mine. It is all about what I've observed in myself and others when it comes to caring, or not caring for others. I've learned to become a more caring person by suffering through all the times I was uncaring. I've learned to become a more caring person by watching others who care well. And I've learned to care better from the examples of those who have cared so well for me.

You will not find five steps to this or eight steps to that within these pages. If you prefer "how-to" books, you're probably better off reading something like Fred Astaire's *Seven Steps to Mastering the Hokey-Pokey—That's What It's All About*. What you'll read here instead are stories of caring that have lifted me out of my narrow, self-centered, all-about-me world to see the richness of life found in caring for others.

* * * * *

I'll start with a story about our son Michael, and what I learned from him. When Michael was a boy, he was hard to read sometimes. I'd ask him questions and he'd give one-word answers. Or he'd grunt, as boys are known to do. The older he got, the more he wanted to talk only on his terms, when he was ready, not necessarily when I was. As with most people, Michael is like a house. Every house has multiple openings. All kinds of openings—windows, doors, chimneys, even clothes-dryer vents. Openings to bring the outside in, or openings to let the inside out.

When you walk past some houses, the resident of the house will see you from inside through a window, open the door and come bounding out to greet you.

"Why don't you come in and I'll get you something to drink. Please stay a while so we can chat and get caught up with each other's lives. I've been thinking about you. I have so much to tell you since we last met. It is so good to see you."

This is how some people respond when we walk past their houses. Such people are wide-open houses with openings that invite you in. They are easy people to engage with—the low-hanging fruit of relationships. It doesn't take a lot of work to relate with people like this. Me, I get along great with children and older ladies because they are houses with relational openings I can easily pick out. Younger than eight and older than eighty is my sweet spot. With everyone in between, not so much.

"What did you do in school today?" or "Tell me about your toy." Both are openings to the house of the less-than-8-year-olds who almost always open the door to their world. It's a little different though, with the greater-than-80 bunch.

"How's that hip of yours doing?" or "Is it my imagination, but do winters seem a lot colder now than years ago?"

Other people are houses with fewer openings. Walk past someone's house like this and when she sees you from her front window, she closes the drapes, pulls the blinds, and turns off the lights. If you go to her front door and ring the doorbell, she'll pretend she's not home and leave you standing there like a rebuffed Jehovah's Witness.

A number of years ago, the elders from a church in our area called me into a meeting to ask me how they could better care for their pastor, who was going through a rough time. Their question showed me they didn't know him very well. The better we know someone, the easier it is to care for them.

I responded to their question with, "I think you need to get to know him better."

"We've tried, but it's hard because he plays it close to the vest. He doesn't let anyone in," replied one of the elders.

His house is full of closed doors and covered windows. The opening to his house is hard to find, but if you work at it long and hard enough, you'll find it.

"Maybe he plays it close to the vest because he's been hurt in the past with being more open, and he doesn't want to be hurt again. Maybe he plays it close to the vest because he doesn't trust you."

A few heads nodded, but that's as far as it went. Some people have closed houses like this. I'm like this myself at times. I play it close to the vest when I don't trust people either. I close the openings to my house to protect myself, which Christian psychologist Larry Crabb calls the most common sin of us all—self-protection. I also tend to shut down when many people are talking, or when just one person is talking who takes over the air waves. I don't like to fight for air time. I tend to close many of the openings to my house if people cut me off in mid-sentence, or quickly redirect the conversation toward something related to them.

Other people have houses whose openings will close up at first, but who wait to see if you come back, and then if the stars are properly aligned, and they've finished watching *Dancing with the Stars*, will crack open the door and whisper to you, "Now is not a good time, maybe next week. I'm not feeling well right now." So you leave with a small opening for the future, a little hope.

Still other people, when they see you come by, will call out from the window, "I'd really like to talk, but the baby is napping, and my husband thinks I spend too much time with my girlfriends, so could you please come back tomorrow? Come at night, though, and come to the back door. I really need to talk to you."

Get the picture? People are like houses with many different openings. Some are wide open, and others closed shut like a lake cottage in the dead of winter. The frustrating thing for me is that I often want to enter a person's relational house through the opening I want, through an easy opening like the front door. I don't want to have to come back again and again, or wait until spring. I don't want to go to the back door at night. I don't want to talk through the screen of the kitchen window, or get on the ground and whisper through the basement window.

But the fact is, if I want to relate well with someone, I have to go with the opening that person gives me, not the one I want. This principle is especially true in caring for others. We can't care well for people if we don't know them very well. To care well means at times we have to pursue people and look for openings to get to know a person at a heart level. It's not always easy, for some people have closed up many of the openings to their house. We can't give up, though. It's important that we work at it. For in the end, it's always worth it.

Our son Michael, for example, didn't give us a lot of openings as a kid. But in time, I learned what Janet had discovered. "I notice when I drive the kids back and forth to school, and Michael is in the front seat next to me, he tends to be more verbal than at other times."

Hmm. Staring straight ahead in the front passenger seat while riding in the car. No eye contact. Both son and parent staring straight ahead in meaningful conversation. Certainly not the opening I would prefer, but if I want to relate to him on terms comfortable for him, I can't be picky. I have to go with the opening he gives me. I think I can do this.

I found by going with the opening he gives me—which would earn both of us an F in Interpersonal Communication 101—I can have meaningful conversation with one of the most important people in my life. I can find out what's going on in his heart, what weighs him down, what lifts him up. Yeah, I think I can do this. So I gave it a try.

The staring-straight-ahead-where-I-don't-have-to-look-at-you opening applied to other areas with Michael, not just in riding in the car. As he grew older in high school and in college, we had meaningful conversations at baseball games. Both of us watching the game in our staring-straight-ahead-where-I-don't-have-to-look-at-you posture.

I loved going to baseball games with Michael. It was when I first realized the joy of having a son who knew more about something than I did. The joy of having a son with expertise in something I only had passing knowledge of. The joy of having a son more capable and competent than I am. He was an all-conference first baseman in high school, played one year in college, and thoroughly enjoyed the strategy and technique of playing the nation's past time well.

I've learned a lot from him, and still do, in our staring-straight-ahead-where-I-don't-have-to-look-at-you conversations. Like when to hit the cutoff man from the outfield, and when to throw it home; or why it's better to pinch hit a left-handed batter against a right-handed pitcher. And just recently I learned from him what a pitcher is supposed to do when a runner is on third and the batter at the plate is attempting a suicide squeeze bunt (answer: throw at the batter's head—he's less likely to bunt the ball, and the catcher can then tag out the runner coming in from third).

As interesting as those conversations have been, I'll never forget one particular opening he gave me when we were watching a baseball game the time he was home for spring break his junior year in college. While staring straight ahead, and completely out of the blue during a pause in the action, he said to me, "Did you know that at the beginning of every semester, I work like crazy to complete all the assignments and papers due from the course syllabus for the entire semester? It usually takes me about six weeks of non-stop work and studying, and not doing much of anything else. I do that for every class."

"Are you nuts?" was my empathetic, fatherly response. "That thought would never have occurred to me in college, and I was a pretty good student, too. Why on earth would you do that?"

"Because I thought, 'What if I got sick during the semester and couldn't finish the course work? I might lose my scholarship.' But I've come to realize it's a control issue. I wanted to take control of my circumstances. I've found that I have a whole lot less control over things than I thought I had. I know I have to trust God more for things like this."

I sat speechless.

It was breathtaking. More so than the Grand Canyon or Niagara Falls. What parent doesn't want to hear this profound realization about life and God from their twenty-year-old son? And all because he opened up his house to me on his terms, not mine.

Michael married shortly after he graduated. Several years after that, he and his wife Hope sat us down one Sunday afternoon and gave us a card announcing "We're having a baby!" And then quickly after the initial surprise, they handed us another card that read "And we're having another baby!" Twins.

Born eight weeks premature, the boys were named George and Grant. These grandsons of ours have also taught me much about how people, even children, are like houses. They open themselves up to us when they want in ways they want—not at the time or manner I prefer.

On the occasions Janet and I have picked them up from school because their parents were away, I've wanted to understand how their day went. What did they learn in kindergarten today? What is going on in their little hearts. I want to know because I love them deeply and want to enter into their world. When I try to get into their "house," they are often very closed. They pull the blinds and turn off the lights with their favorite response, "It's classified."

It's classified? Please, don't they know who I am? I've changed their diapers, which should entitle me to more than, "It's classified, Grandpa." They closed one of the openings to their house I was trying to enter. I wondered if there is another opening they would give me? There was.

I discovered the opening one night when Janet and I were babysitting and it came time to put them to bed. They got their pajamas on, brushed their teeth, and crawled into bed. I then read them a book.

"Can you read another one? Please? Oh please!"

"I need a glass of water."

"Where's my Star Wars guy? I have to look for it. I can't go to sleep without it! Really, I won't fall asleep without it!"

Typical bed-time stall routines. I've been through all of this many times, but then one night, Grant, firmly tucked in bed with the covers up to his chin, pulled out from his arsenal of sleep delaying tactics, this question, "Grandpa, are you going to die?"

Has someone been talking to this boy? Does he know something I don't know?

Ironically, his question came eerily close to the question too frightening for all of our family just six years earlier, "Is *Grant* going to die?" More about that later.

As I sat down on Grant's bed and looked into his eyes, I could tell he had moved from stalling at bedtime, to a deep metaphysical issue mankind has pondered for centuries. I was not prepared for his question, nor for such an opportunity to see into his heart. Grant was giving me an opening to his house, and I wanted to take advantage of it. I can't afford to miss this one, I thought, even though it came at night when I am least alert. But there he was, opening his house to me in a way that worked for him.

As I sat on the bed, I told him, "Yes, I will die someday, but it most likely wouldn't happen for a very long time." I went on to tell him that when I did die, I would go to heaven to be with Jesus, where I would wait for him—to join me many years later. I told Grant we have nothing to worry about when it comes to dying if we know Jesus. For if we know Jesus, we will spend forever with Him and with all the other people who know Him.

A smile broke out on his small lips that told me he was okay with my answer. He could now call it a day because his question about the destiny of mankind was settled and he could move on. He was comforted, as was I.

"Good night, Grant. I love you."

"I love you, too, Grandpa."

I turned out his light, thankful for the opening he had given me to his house, to his heart. We connected at an unwelcome, unexpected time for me. I found with our grandkids some of the most significant conversations I've had with them happened at night sitting on their bed, because it is when it is most comfortable for them. It's when they were the most reflective. I have to be on guard, to be aware, so I can take advantage of the openings they give me.

On another occasion, I was putting George to bed, and started to pray with him by beginning with, "Dear God, I pray for Jennifer…"

"For JENNIFER, Grandpa!?" At which point, he broke into hilarious laughter. "You were praying for Aunt Jennifer!"

Putting our daughter Jennifer—George and Grant's aunt—down for the night years ago was such a part of my routine that I had substituted her name for George's because I was so very tired this particular night. This only served to energize George and give him a second wind to stay awake longer. And as annoying as that was, it did remind me of the significant conversations I had with my own children while sitting on their bed before they drifted off to sleep.

One such conversation that sticks out in my mind happened when Jennifer was about nine years old. We had moved to a new house in June, and it was now September and her first few days at a new school. On this particular night, there came a time in our conversation when Jennifer became especially quiet. With covers pulled up over her chin, I noticed a few tears slowly leaking out of the corners of her eyes. Jennifer rarely shed tears, so I knew this was significant. It was an opening to her house that I know she was reluctant to give me.

As we talked, I discovered her tears came from a place in her heart where loneliness and isolation dwell. She told me that as the new kid in school, she sat alone at lunch in the cafeteria.

My sadness for her was exceeded only by gratitude for the opening she was giving me. I am no stranger to loneliness either. We are close acquaintances. As we talked, more tears flowed from her eyes. I didn't want to miss this opening to share what thirty-some years of dealing with my own loneliness have taught me, but I didn't want to minimize her pain. I remember saying, "Jennifer, let's pray that God will bring you a friend at your new school." She nodded her head in agreement.

Within a few days God did bring her a friend. As Jennifer grew and matured, I remember referring back to this conversation on her bed as a marker in her life. It was part of her history with God that she could go back to when she had a deep need and couldn't fill it on her own. And it all started with a conversation while I sat on her bed, going with the opening she gave me to her house, to her heart.

* * * * *

As significant as the bedside conversations I had with Grant, George, and Jennifer, another bedside conversation I had as a ten-year-old boy myself with my own mother had an even more profound effect on my life for the next thirty years.

It all started with the opening my mother gave me to her house, to a significant part of her past, unknown to me, but which intertwined with mine. What she told me had several layers to it, starting with , "There's a part of my past, and your past, that you need to know about now." Mixed in with maybe, "This will motivate you to behave." And finally, "It's about time I get this off my chest."

What she said came at me like a bucket of cold water thrown in my face. So out of the blue, out of nowhere, so unimaginable and surprising that I did not know what to do with it. As a ten-year-old boy, there was no place to file what she told me. No drawer, no folder, no shelf to store this on. It just plopped itself there on my heart, like a heavy slab of ice.

If a ten-year-old could have heart attack symptoms, like feeling an elephant is sitting on my chest, that would be me. In the days ahead, this elephant-like slab of ice on my heart began to melt, and find its way into my heart, and from there out into my bloodstream, organs, and finally, into every cell in my body.

I would rather not have known this opening to her house, but she could no longer hide it from me. What she told me of her past and my past became the filter through which I viewed my place in the world for the next three decades.

After our conversation was over I sat stunned on my bed, not knowing what would come next, except that life would never be the same from this point on.

Chapter 2

What if the Worst that People Think About Me is True?

Be yourself. Everybody else is taken.
—Oscar Wilde

It was a hot July afternoon when my mother walked into my bedroom, closed the door, and sat down on my brother's bed across from me. Joe and I had matching twin beds with beige bedspreads featuring rows of red-shirted cowboys riding on white horses. With one hand holding the reins, and the other circling a lasso in the air, these cowboys were a picture of the modern-day equivalent of texting while driving. You would have thought the Wild West would have rules about this kind of thing. Or at least you'd think helmets for cowboys would have been mandatory.

I would much rather have been outside playing baseball with my brother Joe and the other boys in our neighborhood. We'd play baseball from early morning until dusk. Our field of preference was the vacant land behind Squeaky Spangenburg's house. I can't remember Squeaky's real name, or even how he came to be known as Squeaky.

The reason I was in my bedroom, while my friends and brother played baseball, was because I had to practice my accordion. Yeah, that's right, an accordion. When I tell this story to people, more often than not, they laugh when they hear the word "accordion." Something inside me wants to defend the accordion. I hear it's making a comeback, and a part of me wants to lead the charge for its resurgence. When

I see others playing the accordion, they are either really old and nerdy—or they're under thirty with a European punk-rock look to them.

I got into the accordion thing because a music store came to the Catholic grade school I attended and lent the school about a dozen miniature accordions. They hoped to get kids interested in the instrument. I got into a group with these small, cheap, rental accordions and started to take free group lessons at school. This was back in the late 1950s and the only thing I can remember about our group was a girl named Rita on whom I had a crush. She always wore a plain white t-shirt that stood in stark contrast to her jet-black hair. The other attraction to Rita was her parents' big, new, gray '58 Buick with large tail fins. Our family came from the used Chevy side of the tracks, so I held in awe anyone who came from a family who owned a new Buick.

The free accordion rental at school ended after a short time, and then parents had to start paying for the rental, and also for private lessons. Surprisingly, my parents bought into this. I got the sense they were pushing me to get really good at it so I could make money some day, playing for weddings, dances, and maybe become the next Myron Florin on *The Lawrence Welk Show*. Man, I hated that show. Every Saturday night.

They signed me up for lessons, and every Saturday morning, Conrad Kish would come to our house to give me lessons. He must have only been twenty years old or so, and told us to call him Connie, an odd name for a guy, unless you were Connie Mack, the famous baseball manager of the old Philadelphia Athletics. Connie Kish came to our house in his late-model, two-tone beige Plymouth and did the best he could to teach me to play. He was a very hip looking kind of guy, so the accordion and the "Connie" didn't quite seem to fit.

I soon learned that to please Connie and my parents, I had to practice, which I didn't mind much at first. But there came a time when he had a talk with my parents about how I was outgrowing the cheap miniature accordion, and I needed to get a real standard-issue one if I was going to make any progress. Money, though, was always tight around our house. I remember my parents fighting over it all the time. There were seven of us in the family and my dad's factory job as a foreman and supervisor apparently didn't pay enough to keep us all comfortable.

One day, when I came home from school, there it was, a new accordion. A new official-sized, red accordion adults play, with all the keys and all the buttons. More buttons than I knew how to play at the time. I didn't care much for the red, but the fact it was an official major league adult model outweighed the color. It was a used one that worked fine, but I would have preferred a black one like everyone else had. I was the only kid I knew who had a red accordion. As a ten-year old, I hated being different about anything. And this red accordion made me different.

What my mother was about to tell me, however, made playing a red accordion seem as common as a field of yellow dandelions in late spring. I must have been complaining about practicing that afternoon, knowing my brother and all our friends were playing baseball. She had heard enough from me—the grousing and whining about practicing.

Separated only by the sheet music for *The Marines' Hymn* resting on my folding metal music stand, and my red accordion on my lap, she folded her hands in her lap on top of the threadbare apron she always wore and said, "I want you to stop your complaining about wanting to go outside and play. I'm sick of hearing it. That accordion of yours cost us a lot of money. And, besides that, ah, ... your dad isn't your real father. He didn't have to buy it for you, but he did. So you should be grateful. And the least you can do is practice it!"

Gulp. I was shocked into silence.

Recovering from this stunning revelation, I asked, "What do you mean, he isn't my real father?"

"Your real father was a truck driver who lived in Indiana and came up to Milwaukee to deliver empty beer cans to one of the breweries. He and I would see each other when he was in town. Then one day, you were born."

"Well, what? I mean, really? Ah, did he support us?"

"No." And then very agitated, with a nervous voice and wringing hands, she rose from my brother's bed and said, "When I wrote to tell him I was pregnant with you, he told me he couldn't support us because he already had a family of his own in Indiana. I never saw him after that. I worked at the telephone company during the day, then served drinks at night at a bowling alley to support us. I lived with two of my girlfriends and that's how we got by until I met your dad. After we got married, he adopted you."

Leaving the room, she parted with, "Now get back to practicing your accordion. I don't want to hear another word out of you!"

* * * * *

I don't think Mom would have done well as a motivational speaker. A career as a child psychologist wouldn't have suited her either. I imagine, though, she must have been relieved to tell me about our past. I wonder what it was like for her to hold so much in for the past ten years. The shame. The angst. The embarrassment. *When do I tell him? Do I ever tell him at all? Does he really need to know?* All questions I wonder if she struggled with. I don't know, because she died in 2003, before I had a chance to ask her. So many other questions have risen since she's been gone that I'll never know the answers to.

What was a ten-year-old boy supposed to do with the information my mother just dropped in my lap like a 500-pound anvil? Mastering *Camptown Races* on my accordion wasn't going to help. Such confusion. Inside, it felt like I was silently walking around with arms outstretched and mouth wide open looking for answers. *What does this all mean? Who am I now?*

I have kids and grandkids of my own, so I know what it's like when they whine and complain about something they need to do—even something they agreed to do, as I did when I said I would practice my accordion if my parents would let me take lessons. But even using guilt to stop my grousing, and how I should be grateful for my father—my stepfather—for buying the accordion didn't work to make me practice. Neither did marrying my mom, adopting me, and rescuing both of us. None of this worked to keep me playing for much longer. I wanted to play baseball instead.

My parents later sold the accordion, and while that part of my life soon was gone, the disclosure of the circumstances surrounding my birth have never left me. Over the next thirty years, I would think about it more than I ever wanted, and when I wasn't thinking about it, it seemed like it was thinking about me. It secretly moved into my heart. And every so often out of the blue, it would whisper to me, "You know, you should never have been born. That's not how it works. How you came into the world is not how it's done. There's a reason they call people like you 'illegitimate.'"

I majored in history in college, where I learned about William the Conqueror, the French duke who invaded England in 1066. He is most famous as coming out the victor in the Battle of Hastings. His contemporaries referred to him as "Duke William the Bastard." *The what? Really?* He had been born out of wedlock like me. I wonder if it affected his identity as much as it had mine.

My father—my stepfather—threw the B word around the house all the time when he was angry at me. He used it in complaining about the suits at work who would invade his territory on the factory shop floor, much like Duke William the Conqueror—William the Bastard— invaded Normandy. I grew numb to his profanity, for the more I heard it, the more it became part of normal.

But it wasn't until I learned of Duke William and what people called him that it dawned on me that when my father called me the B word, it was more than just an expression of his profane anger. He was calling me literally what I was. It made my stomach sink and churn. I wonder what it had done to Duke William. He at least conquered England. Me? I couldn't conquer my own sense of confusion and dread over who I was.

What did it mean? For more years than I care to admit, it meant everything. Now, most days—except on some of my birthdays—it means nothing.

I see other people with identity issues of their own. Poor self-esteem. Lack of confidence. Trying to prove something to someone (often a dead person). Working to earn a parent's or spouse's love. I have come to appreciate the question, "So what if the worst about us is true?" If what people say about us is something we can change? Well then, have at it. Make those changes. If not, so what? Instead of working hard to change people's minds, just accept who we are as someone made by God, wired and gifted in the way he designed us, and nurture that identity, instead of trying to change it.

So much emotional energy is wasted trying to prove people wrong about us. When Conan O'Brien was forced out of his dream job, host of *The Tonight Show*, he commented "There's nothing as freeing as when your worst fear is realized." I so agree. Sometimes when people bemoan how terrible a person they are, I find myself thinking, "Why does this surprise you?" We are all terrible. So why fight it? Do what you can. Change behaviors and attitudes that are in your power to change. But please, stop trying so hard to be someone you're not.

Many people are consumed much more with who they are than who you are. The more we know who we are—the good, the bad, and the ugly—the greater will be our capacity to love and to be the caring kind of person God wants us to be. So enough with the worrying about what other people think.

Too many of us give a lot of power to other people to define us. What others think of us often becomes way too important. I like hanging around people who have a grounded sense of who they are, and are not swayed by the judgment of others. One really great example of this is a story from the Book of Acts in the Bible. Near the end of the book in Chapter 28, the Apostle Paul becomes shipwrecked off the island of Malta. He and the others on the ship manage to get to shore safely where he says, "The islanders showed us unusual kindness." I love this phrase, *unusual kindness.*

Paul builds a fire along the shore of Malta "because it was rainy and cold." While he is doing so, a snake jumps out of the wood pile used to fuel the fire and latches onto his arm. Seeing this, the people of Malta cry out, "He must be a murderer!" Snakes grabbing onto your arm were apparently a sure sign you were a criminal. Uncharacteristically, Paul says nothing in his defense and instead grabs the snake from his arm and throws it into the fire.

The islanders wait a while and nothing happens to Paul. His arm doesn't swell up; he doesn't die from snake bite. Perplexed, the people in the crowd change their minds and shout, "He must be a god!" Poor Paul, his approval rating rose, fell, and rose again like a yo-yo. He ignored both the complaints of his critics and the praise of his fans.

I love this story on several levels. It shows how fickle people can be. The people of Malta go from "unusual kindness" to "he's a murderer" to "he must be a god." I also love how Paul responds to them. He says nothing, which is so unlike him. In many places throughout the Book of Acts, and the letters he writes to churches recorded in the New Testament, he defends himself against attacks on his credibility. But here he chooses to remain silent, and not defend himself.

One could make a case that Paul was indeed a murderer. Prior to his conversion, he sought out Christians to put to death; he didn't pull the trigger, but he was certainly responsible for the death of many believers. He stood by and watched while Stephen was murdered, for example. But Paul knew who he was, warts and all. And murdering people is a mighty big wart. Yet that sordid part of his past didn't incapacitate him. If it were me, I would have wilted and been drawn back to that ugly time in my life I wish had never happened. Not Paul. Rather than letting his past define him, rather than allowing his unregenerate background label him, he let the past be the past. What he was before isn't nearly as important as who he was now.

Paul knew he could be considered a murderer, but he also knew he was forgiven and reconciled with God through his relationship with God's son, Jesus Christ. His identity was now in Christ, and what he did in the past was no longer of any consequence. God forgave him through the sacrifice of His son on the cross.

As with me, Paul knew there was something seriously wrong with himself. But it didn't matter because he was now playing to an audience of one—God. It was only what God thought that mattered.

Paul moved forward from the past to be the person God called him to be in the present. He let the Maltese islanders think whatever they wanted of him. He let them be wrong with their assessment of him, and he moved on. The worst about him was known and it didn't matter. It enabled Paul to live in the here and now with freedom. He didn't have to prove himself to anyone.

Nothing to prove; nothing to lose.

The story of Paul's shipwreck off Malta ends with Paul ignoring the opinions of others and going about what God called him to do. He went to the home of the chief official of the island and healed the official's father, followed by healing other people on the island who were sick.

What a great example of having a firm understanding of who we are. What a great example of self-awareness and not falling victim to our past and letting it define us. What a great example of doing what God has called us to do, regardless of what our critics may say about us.

This freedom of "nothing to prove, nothing to lose" enabled Paul to extend himself to others in being a more caring and compassionate man.

So if a murderer like Paul can move beyond his past to care for people, maybe there's hope for a someone born out of wedlock to care for people and to reflect well the image of God. Yeah, there's something wrong with Paul, and me. But so what? There is something wrong with everyone. There's too much of life to live to be influenced by the power we give our critics, most of whom do not know us very well. There's too much of life to enjoy and find fulfillment in, even if the worst that people say about us is true. It takes too much emotional energy to defend ourselves. Getting caught up in pleasing people and not accepting who we are keeps us from caring well for others. Why should what others think of me be so important?

For me, the answer to this question has not come easily. To live in the freedom of knowing that even if the worst that people could think about me is true has taken me nearly forty years to resolve. It doesn't matter what they think; it only matters what God thinks. Coming to this simple, but profound, conclusion only came at the end of a difficult journey for me. A difficult search to fill in the blanks to find the missing pieces from my mother's "he's not your REAL father" story told me on that hot July afternoon when I was ten years old. Joining me at the start of this journey was my friend Bill.

Chapter 3

Courthouse Secrets

*There is something about a closet
that makes a skeleton terribly restless.*
—John Barrymore

My friend Bill was a lot different from me. Old enough to be my father, but unlike me, there wasn't much of anything wrong with Bill. He was one of the kindest men I have ever known. By the time we first met Bill and his wife, they had raised a family, while family raising was still a work in progress for Janet and me.

Bill always carried a pen and a very small note pad with his to-do list in his shirt pocket, something his family would sometimes make fun of. He would laugh at their reaction while he touted the benefits of being organized and prepared. I admired how comfortable Bill was in his own skin.

After his wife, Dorothy, died, Bill lived a full and productive life. But then he developed prostate cancer, and I watched him die. His daughters lovingly cared for him in his home, and my wife Janet would spend nights with Bill and his daughters so none of them would be alone. No one should be alone when they die.

I took a shift being with Bill one night, and in the midst of small talk and watching TV, he looked to me and said, "I want to thank you for all that you have meant to our family, for how you've blessed Dorothy and me, and how you've been good friends to our children."

It was his good-bye to me. Bill was a class act. I miss him dearly.

He was logical, gentle, very organized, and always assumed the best about people. Me? Not so much. Our personalities were as different as our ages. But it was our differences that drew me to Bill, because more often than not, I find people who are different from me much more interesting.

One day Bill told me he was starting to get interested in his family history. He wanted to learn more about where he came from and then pass this information down to his children and grandchildren. To help with this, Bill decided to attend a meeting of the Milwaukee Genealogical Society at the main library downtown, and he wanted to know if I would like to come with him.

I wanted to know where I came from, too, particularly as it related to my birth father, the man who brought me into this world in a one-night stand with my mother. The man who abandoned us and who made life very difficult for my farm-girl mother from Staples, Minnesota. The man who was having a greater and greater unwelcome influence in my life, though we had never met. Discovering who he was might help me discover who I was.

So with all this in mind, I decided to go with Bill. Plus I've always wanted to be part of a society. Bill knew I just wanted to track down my birth father, while he wanted to track down all his relatives. We were both okay with our differing, but related, goals. We went to the first meeting and both of us became hooked on discovering our roots. This was in the early 1990s, before the Internet was widely available, so playing family detective and historian was a bit more challenging than it is today.

While I focused on the search for my birth father, I was conflicted about my stepfather. He was very warm, generous, and engaging with other people, but not with me. We were not close. I don't think he knew what to do with me. I remember him always being displeased, a little irritated with me. He discouraged me from going to college and said I would never make it.

"You're not college material," he would say. I remember him drinking and making my mother cry when he came home drunk. He never hit her, but he would hit me on occasion. Sometimes, when we were all in the car driving somewhere, I worried we would be killed in a car accident, especially at night. I remember praying to God that He would postpone that tragic event until at least after I got to see my first major league baseball game at Milwaukee County Stadium. God answered that prayer, and one other very important prayer I will tell you about later.

My mother told me he was not my real father, yet in every sense of the word, he was a real father to me. A flawed, imperfect father, but a father nevertheless. We lacked a biologic connection, but he was still the man who pursued my mother and married her in spite of the fact I was part of the package. He was the father who, together with my mother, raised me and provided for my material needs. He was the father who bought a used red accordion for me when they had little money to spare. He was the father who taught me things, like how to fly a kite, throw a curveball, and ice skate. He was the father who took my brother, sisters, and me sledding on cold winter afternoons.

I wish I would have learned more from him, like how to play tennis and sheepshead, as he had a reputation for excelling in both. The other father, my birth father, taught me nothing and provided me nothing. I don't like the step-thing, so when I speak of Harry Certalic, the man who raised me, I'm going to stick with "Father." To call him anything less would be disrespectful. He deserves better.

The other father? I don't know what to call him.

* * * * *

From the time my mother first told me I was born out of wedlock and later adopted by my father, I wondered a lot about who my biological father was, and a lot about who I was. I always felt different as a kid. I was taller than my siblings, and as a teenager, was much taller than my parents. Maybe the circumstances surrounding my birth explained why I was depressed much of the time growing up.

"How you came into the world is not how it's done. You never should have been born" was a feeling that kept repeating itself over and over again in my soul, like a song on a damaged CD that skips because of a scratched track. Maybe if I knew more about my birth father and where I came from, I would be less depressed.

Long before attending the Milwaukee Genealogical Society meetings with Bill, I began the search for the mystery man from my past. One morning, when I was twenty years old and home from college, I sat at the kitchen table of our small house, just with my mother and father, as my brother and sisters were in school. Fighting back my fear of not knowing what would happen next, I summoned all the courage I could muster to continue the conversation my mother started with me ten years earlier.

"Mom, do you remember when I was about ten and you told me Dad was not my natural father? I was wondering whatever happened to my…"

With that, my father quickly jumped up from the table, forcefully cutting me off and pounding his fist on the kitchen table next to his coffee cup, blurting out, "He was a truck driver and was killed in an accident. That's all we're ever going to talk about this!"

Something inside told me he was not telling the truth as he stormed out of the room.

For the next twenty years, I wondered about that conversation. Especially around the time of my birthday. I could never enjoy my birthday, for it would once again bring up the "how you came into the world is not how it's done; you never should have been born" theme from the basement of my heart. It would start a cycle of depression that would last for several days. I felt like crawling in a hole and just sleeping until the depression lifted, as it always did with time. I felt so different from the rest of the world. *Why can't I be just like everyone else?* Yet part of me was glad I was not like everyone else. But that part, the missing-legitimacy-to-my-birth part, was where I wanted to be like everyone else. The mystery about my origins troubled me deeply.

I read with rapt attention newspaper articles about people reuniting with their birth parents. I intently watched TV shows and movies about children discovering as adults, siblings they never knew they had. There'd be scenes in the airport with middle-aged people hugging their newly found brothers and sisters as they got off the plane. Maybe there's someone out there like that for me. Maybe my biological father had always wondered about me and was trying to track me down. Maybe if I knew more about where I had come from, I would be less depressed. Maybe.

In the genealogy classes Bill and I attended, we learned how to find valuable information from public records, like birth certificates filed in courthouses. The copy of my birth certificate shows my last name is Certalic and my father is Harry Certalic. Nothing unusual about this, except if I had been adopted by Harry Certalic, why did his name appear on my birth certificate? My mother told me they married a year and a half after I was born and that he didn't adopt me until I was five. Were my parents lying to me? Was the conversation my mother had with me when I was ten, about being illegitimate and rescued by my father, really just a ruse to get me to practice that red accordion? It made me angry to think about it. What are they not telling me? Why can't people tell me the truth?

Things became a bit clearer when I went to our local courthouse to see what they had on me. I found a large ledger book where births in

Milwaukee County were recorded in chronological order. I went to the day I was born and looked for my name with the other births recorded for the day. I found my name, and everything appeared in order, except for one entry—my last name. It clearly showed my last name, "Certalic," but under the ink appeared some primitive form of Wite-Out, covering over what had originally been entered. It was quite obvious someone had erased what was recorded as my surname, and then wrote "Certalic" over the erasure. What is this cover-up all about?

I learned through the genealogy class that in Wisconsin, when a child is adopted, its original birth certificate is impounded and a new one issued with the name of the adopted parent(s) shown. So that explains why my official birth certificate looks normal, but the ledger book at the courthouse has the erasure. All this to protect the confidentiality of the birth parent(s). While I'm all for confidentiality in most areas of life, what about the right of children to know who brought them into the world?

Who really, then, was my birth father? What name was covered over on the court ledger? What did my original birth certificate look like? As I neared my 40th birthday, I became more and more agitated and depressed about the whole thing. Janet kept encouraging me to talk to my mother to get more information. The last conversation I had on the topic hadn't gone very well, so I was not anxious to open a can of worms with her again.

But one Sunday afternoon while visiting my parents, I summoned the courage to try to finish the conversation of twenty years ago about my origins. This in itself was an attempt to finish the conversation begun ten years before. I had been dealing with this whole thing for thirty years, and not dealing with it very well. The voices whispering in my heart, "How you came into the world is not how it's done; you never should have been born," grew louder and more frequent.

By then, my father had suffered a paralyzing stroke several years after retiring from his factory job. Because of his stroke, he spent most of his time in a wheelchair watching TV. So with him in the living room, and my mother in the kitchen out of ear shot, I continued my conversation with my mom from twenty years ago. In the same room, the same conversation.

"Mom, do you remember when I was ten and you told me Dad was not my real father? Who was my natural father?"

She told me some of what she had said before at that time, that he was a truck driver living in Indiana who would deliver empty beer cans to one of the breweries in town.

"Did he support us?"

"No, when I asked for money to help us, he said he couldn't because he had a family of his own in Indiana he had to support."

With a tight grimace in her face and shoulders hunched up, she continued, "And that's the last I ever talked to him, that b-----d."

"What was his name?"

"Jack Byrd.

"Where in Indiana did he live?

"Fort Wayne."

"I want to try and track him down, Mom. Do you want to know what I find out."

"No."

* * * * *

Something inside of me told me he might still be alive. The fact my mother mentioned nothing about him being killed in a traffic accident, as my father had twenty years before, confirmed even more my suspicions they may not have been truthful to me back then. When my mother told me my biological father's name was Jack Byrd from

Fort Wayne, Indiana, my heart both sank and leaped at the same time. The former, because I thought there must be thousands of Jack Byrds in the world, the latter, because as I came to learn from the class I was taking, Fort Wayne has one of the best genealogy libraries in the country.

Jack Byrd. Fort Wayne, Indiana. Lived there in 1948. That's all I had to go on.

At the time of the conversation with my mother, our son and daughter were attending Grace College in Winona Lake, Indiana— interestingly enough, about forty miles from Fort Wayne. I thought I could extend one of our weekend trips to visit our kids by driving to Fort Wayne to try locating this Jack Byrd. Rather than waiting for our next trip, I wanted to get going on the research soon. But without the Internet, and certainly without Google, I didn't have a lot to go on.

While at home, I started with directory assistance. (My apologies here to the thirty and younger crowd. Ask your parents or grandparents about "directory assistance.") I called the Fort Wayne area code, asking for the phone number of any Jack Byrd, of which there were three. Each with different middle names or initials. So I called my mother and asked here if she remembered his middle name, and she did —it was Edward. *Jack Edward Byrd.* So I called the only Jack E. Byrd listed with directory assistance and found out he wasn't the Byrd I was looking for.

This Jack Byrd told me, "Back in the 1950s, I used to get mistaken for him all the time. Bill collectors and other people kept calling me, thinking I was the other Jack E. Byrd. It was quite annoying. Sorry I can't help you out, but good luck in finding him."

Starting this search process surprised me; something I had ignored for thirty years had developed into a sense of urgency to locate my birth father. It created an adrenaline rush in me that lasted for about six months. In the genealogy class I learned of services that track down birth parents for adopted children. So I contacted one and paid twenty-five dollars for them to try locating Jack Edward Byrd. They came up with nothing. *They're not trying hard enough*, I thought.

I then pushed up the date to visit our college kids. It was 1991 and we decided to visit them over their homecoming weekend in October. We went down on a Thursday evening. On Friday, while Janet spent time with our daughter Jennifer and our son Michael in Winona Lake, I drove over to Fort Wayne. I wanted to use what I had been learning to try locating the mystery man in my life.

My first stop was the Allen County Public Library in Fort Wayne, where I camped out in the Genealogical Department. Looking through every source I could think of, I documented my research as I used to do when I wrote term papers in college. Using one bit of information to lead to another energized me. I started looking through the obituary notices from the Fort Wayne newspaper. Found nothing there. I had to move on to something different, and to do it quickly, for I was due back in Winona Lake the same evening to attend homecoming activities with our kids.

Checking out city directories, I found listings for Jack E. Byrd from 1946 to 1955. His employers indicated several trucking firms he worked for during this period. He disappeared after that. I looked for current listings of these same trucking companies, but they did not exist anymore. Had they still been in business, maybe an old-timer there would have remembered my birth father. Time was running out and I still hadn't gotten the information I needed. Maybe I'll have to come back and visit the addresses where he lived in the early 1950s to see if any of the neighbors were there at the time, and if so, ask if they knew his whereabouts.

With nowhere else to look in the Genealogical Department of the Allen County Library, and with time moving quickly, I went across the street to the Allen County Courthouse. It was there I found a treasure trove of information I needed. Room 201 houses the marriage and divorce records, so I started there. I was surprised, yet not surprised at what I found.

It's amazing what information you can find on a marriage license. I discovered Jack Edward Byrd was born on April 4, 1922. This April 4th date is a very significant date in my own history, which I will get to later. He married a woman named Helen Jane Williamson in 1940. I was pretty sure this was my Jack Edward Byrd because it showed his occupation as a truck driver living in the area.

Piecing together information from later marriage licenses and divorce records, I became convinced this was indeed the Jack Byrd who was my biological father. From his first marriage, a daughter, Judith Ann, was born the same year. This marriage was his first of six, five of which ended in divorce. One ended with the death of his last wife.

At the time of my birth in February 1949 he was on wife number three, and had four children from these marriages. Then there was me. I was conceived the same month his fourth child was born. So he was right in telling my mother when she announced her pregnancy to him that he had another family in Indiana and couldn't support the two of us and his Indiana family at the same time.

I certainly had no illusions my birth father was the epitome of virtue or that Focus on the Family was going to be contacting him anytime soon to present a lifetime achievement award. He was married three more times after I was born. On several of the wedding licenses, I noticed he either lied to whomever recorded the data, or there was a misprint.

The clock was ticking ever faster as I read through all this data. I wrote down names and any possible contact information from documents I discovered that I could later follow up on when I got home. Once I had gotten all there was to get in room 201, I then checked for civil and probate records, but I wasn't very thorough because their indexing system was hard to figure out and there wasn't time to learn it.

I still had about an hour left to do whatever research I could. There was more I could check, but it might have to wait for another trip to Fort Wayne. But the adrenaline was flowing and I wanted to use every minute left. So I went across the street from the courthouse to the city/county building to look for records there. Nothing turned up for Jack E. Byrd, but I did find a few records for his son Timothy Kevin Byrd. First a property deed from 1990, then divorce papers from his wife. I wrote down any names and contact information I could possibly follow up on later.

With lots of paper filled with my notes, I headed back to Winona Lake for the evening homecoming activities with our son and daughter. I had spent the day using what I learned in the genealogy class, as well as what I learned from a summer job when I was a teacher. I worked for an insurance investigation firm where I checked court documents, looking for criminal records and civil actions. Added to this were the skills I developed as a headhunter, where I used one bit of information to lead to another. All of this experience came into play in searching for Jack Edward Byrd. I think I was enjoying this process more than I should have. It gave me a sense of control and power over what had rendered me powerless for so many years.

As part of the evening homecoming activities that night at Grace College, there is a wonderful custom of students writing essays about why their parents should be named "Parents of the Year." The winning essay is then read to a packed auditorium, and the winning parents are ushered on to the stage and given a plaque. We sat through several of these in years past and were always touched by the love of parents for their children, and the appreciation of their children for that love, in whatever manner it was displayed. Moreover, the essays were almost invariably about parents loving their college-aged kids in spite of really difficult obstacles and circumstances in their own lives.

So as the time came near to hear this year's winning essay, the contrast between my own birth father and the type of husband, parent, and man he was, compared to all the previous winners of this wonderful honor, sloshed around in my mind like newly mixed cherry Jello in a bowl ready to be put in the refrigerator. I couldn't get over what all the court records had revealed about that man.

With him on my mind, it was difficult listening to the winning essay being read to the audience, until I suddenly realized what I was hearing could be from no one else but our daughter. I felt all the air rising from my lungs. Janet realized it at the same time and gasped audibly (she does gasps much better than I do). Tears trickled down both our faces and when we glanced over at our daughter, tears were doing a number on her face, too.

Janet and I were that year's "Parents of the Year."

* * * * *

How could this be possible, given my own "parent" I had just spent the day hunting for? Our daughter had nothing to say about great obstacles Janet and I faced in life. Neither of us had cancer, we'd never been in a terrible car accident, nor were we ever held hostage for months by terrorists, nor plagued with crippling birth defects. The closest we could come to people with these debilitating circumstances was a bad case of chapped lips every now and then in the winter.

Yet we still won the award. I don't get it.

It never occurred to me that maybe my mother and stepfather had something to do with it. It never occurred to me Janet's parents might have played a role in her learning to parent well. What did occur to me though, is that God had an awful lot to do with it, and quite possibly he was going to use this event to bring a measure of healing to my soul—

especially in the stark contrast between where I had come from and where I had arrived at this current season of life.

When we got up on stage, we were given a framed piece of beautiful decorative glass, etched with our names, "Parents of the Year—1991." In the days and months that followed, I wondered aloud what other benefits would accrue to Parents of the Year—1991. Courtside seating at the college's basketball game? Nope. A building named after us? No, too many others in line for this. A preferred parking space in the college parking lot? This was already taken by handicapped people and the Student Foodservice Dishwasher of the Month. We were forgotten as quickly as the winner of the World Series three years ago. Which was really just fine.

The award was for the moment, not even for the year, but for the moment, which really was quite sufficient. It was more than we deserved. Treasured moments often last longer than memorable days, weeks, or years. And for me, the treasured moment was hearing what our daughter thought of us and how she took the time from her studies to honor us with what was on her heart. The award was really more about her than about us.

The next year our son wrote a similar essay that he entered. But his wasn't chosen.

"Sorry, Mom and Dad," he said. "I did the best I could."

"Don't worry about it, Michael. You didn't have much to work with. Both Mom and I were still alive, neither one of us divorced the other, we weren't paralyzed in a wheelchair, we didn't lose our job, the house, or the farm."

Maybe if he had played up my chapped lips, he would have had a better chance.

Chapter 4

Getting in the Boat with People

What he needs from you is to be his friend, and then to show up.
—from "The Soloist"

Once we were back home in Milwaukee after my foray into the secrets of the Allen County Courthouse, I organized the notes I had taken and began mapping out a plan to locate Jack E. Byrd. Oh, how I wish Google and whitepages.com had been around then. I told a few friends about my research project, and one couple in particular, Brad and Kathy, asked me every now and then how the search was going. It was energizing to talk about it with them. I felt a sense of control and even power in my quest. Had I to do it over, I think I would have enjoyed being a detective or investigative journalist.

During my search for my birth father, Janet and I went out for dinner with Brad and Kathy every six or eight weeks or so. On one of these occasions, we were seated at a restaurant and after completing our orders, Kathy asked, "So how's it going with the search for your birth father?"

Without warning, I started to weep. My face looked like the basement wall of a house we used to own when very heavy rains sent water trickling down the inside walls. That, of course, is the wrong side for rain water to flow. Tears belong on the outside, too, where they can release what has been building up inside. I had no idea what I had been holding in until the tears started to flow.

Restaurants, however, are not good places to discover pain that has been building for thirty years. But Janet and my friends Brad and Kathy handled it well. They didn't say much. They didn't try to fix me, or stop my tears out of their discomfort at my display. Sometimes doing nothing is the best thing we can do to care for a person. And they cared for me well that night. Their silence created an opportunity for me to talk about what had just happened. When the tears started flowing from my eyes, words began forming in my heart that I could gather together and put in a sentence.

"I feel like I should never have been born. This is not how it's done. I'm finding out how awful Jack Byrd was. All the divorces. All the kids he left behind without a father. What he put my mother through. When I began the search, I had no illusion he was some noble man who would have been a much better father to me than the one who raised me. But this theme of 'I should never have been born' keeps playing and playing."

Janet, Brad, and Kathy didn't try to talk me out of my thinking. They just listened, and their eyes told me they felt badly for me. Their faces told me they hurt for me. And that alone comforted me. There's something within all of us that wants to be known, and they seemed to know what I was going through.

In the weeks that followed, I called directory assistance to get as many phone numbers as possible of people whose names appeared on various documents I found in my research trip to Fort Wayne.

Directory assistance seems so archaic now. Why talk to an actual person when we can press keys on our computers and smartphones instead? Who needs a human being to find information when we have the Internet and Google? But what about all those directory assistance telephone operators? What happened to all of them?

My mother's first job out of high school was as a telephone operator. Maybe we could enact a government stimulus program to re-train directory assistance telephone operators like my mother to become relational assistance operators.

"Hello, Relational Assistance. How may I help you?"

"I am really frustrated with my ten-year-old son. He pleaded with us to take accordion lessons, and though we had reservations about whether he'd really be committed to practice, we signed him up against our better judgment. It was a real sacrifice for us because money is tight and we have four other kids to consider, too. In the beginning, he practiced, but now after about two years, he's not showing the self-discipline he needs. Every time his accordion teacher comes over to give him a lesson, I feel we're flushing money down the toilet because Johnny practices so little between lessons. So how can I get him to practice this summer when all he wants to do is play baseball?"

"I feel your pain, Mrs. Certalic. I can tell you one thing not to do. Even if it's true, don't tell him he needs to practice because of the sacrifice you and your husband made in buying the accordion. Don't tell him he ought to practice out of gratitude, especially considering that the man he thinks is his father isn't his real father, but rather his stepfather who adopted him several years after the two of you got married. Don't tell him his real father had a one-night stand with you and that he couldn't support you and your son because of his real family back in Indiana."

"OK. But if I can't do that, what can I do to get him to practice when he all he wants to do is play baseball all day?"

"Have you tried praying for rain?"

* * * * *

Using directory assistance, I started calling Jack E. Byrd's ex-wives and children, whose names I had found on marriage and divorce records. Several of them were easily located; others I could not find. The ones I could locate were scattered around various communities in Indiana. Unlike their husband and father, they didn't stray far from their Hoosier roots. He, on the other hand, as I discovered, strayed as geographically as he did in his martial relationships, ending up in various cities in Alabama and Florida.

In contacting these people, what I wanted to say was, "Hi, I'm John Certalic. You don't know me and I don't know you. But I'm wondering if you know where I can find Jack E. Byrd—if he's still alive. I'm the result of his getting my mom pregnant with me back in 1948. He left my mom to fend for herself while he went back to his wife and kids in Indiana. So if he's still alive, I want to talk to him because my illegitimate birth has haunted me for thirty years and makes me quite depressed every time I think about it. It makes me depressed even when I'm not thinking about it—especially around the time of my birthday. Do you have a phone number for him?"

That's what I wanted to say. What I didn't want was this skeleton in their family closets to come falling down on them, fracturing something in them like it did me. I didn't want to open a can of worms for them. I didn't want to let the cat out of the bag. I didn't want to use other clichés for this very important process to me. I had to be honest, yet not reveal too much that would arouse suspicion.

So when I called, I would introduce myself and simply say, "I am doing research into my family history and as part of the search, I'm trying to locate a Jack Edward Byrd, someone I think I may be related to. Do you know if he's still alive and if so, what his phone number is?"

No one ever questioned my motives. No one ever asked how I might be related. No one ever asked, "Well, if you think you're related to Jack Byrd, do you think maybe you might be related to me, too?" If they had, I probably would have just hung up the phone without answering. I've learned not every question people ask needs to be answered. I've also learned on the rare occasion when people ask me a question that makes me feel uncomfortable, it helps to ask a question in return, "Why do you ask?"

One particular ex-wife I contacted, a woman living in Rensselaer, Indiana, was most helpful. She had lost track of her ex- a number of years ago, but she had a lot of names and phone numbers of family members who might know the whereabouts of one Jack E. Byrd. She did think he was still alive. I spent many evenings calling these leads and asking each of them for additional leads. Lots of phone calls, but no success. That was okay, though, because I was doing something. I could do, rather than feel. Doing something gave me a measure of control. It quieted the "you never should have been born; it's not how people are supposed to come into the world" voices.

Knowing he quite possibly could still be alive kept my search for Jack E. Byrd alive. One night, while going through my notes from my research in Fort Wayne, I found notes I had scribbled down from the divorce papers of one of Jack Byrd's sons, Timothy Kevin Byrd. I should mention that in my search, I was always asking for leads to any of Jack Byrd's children, thinking they would likely know how to reach their father, if in fact he was still alive. For some unexplainable reason, when I was at the courthouse, I also wrote down the name of the attorney and law firm who handled the divorce for Timothy Kevin Byrd, which took place in the 1980s.

The next day, I called the law firm of that attorney and asked to speak to him. Relieved he was still with them, I explained I was doing some family history research and noticed in some court documents he represented Timothy Kevin Byrd's divorce.

"He is someone I may be related to and I'd like to talk to him. Do you know how I can reach him?"

"Well, if I did, I couldn't tell you—attorney-client privilege and all that. I do remember him, though, and by the way, he goes by Kevin Byrd. I haven't talked to him in years, but the last I heard, he had moved to Ohio."

That explained why I couldn't locate him through directory assistance in the (219) area code in Indiana. In those days, there was no nationwide directory assistance—you had to make a request for a person in a specific city, or at the very least, in a specific area code.

"What about his wife, his ex-wife? Do you know how I can reach her?"

"Hmm. I think she still lives in the Fort Wayne area," he replied.

I had her name from the divorce records so I called directory assistance in Fort Wayne, got her phone number, and then waited a few days before calling. I sensed this call was going to finally lead to where I wanted to go. It felt like I was closing in on a hunt I did not want to end. It was like coming to end of a good book you didn't want to finish, because the pleasure in reading it would also come to an end. That's why I waited before I called.

More nervous than in any of my previous calls, when Kevin Byrd's ex-wife answered the phone I said, "Hi, you don't know me, but my name is John Certalic. I'm doing research into my family history and as part of this, I'm trying to locate a Jack Edward Byrd, someone I think I may be related to. I understand you used to be married to one of his sons, Kevin. Is that correct?"

Then silence. And more silence.

Finally, with a nervous, halting voice, she replied, "Yes, that's correct."

"I'm wondering if I can ask you a few questions about Jack Byrd."

Silence once again on the other end of the line. After a very long pause, she said, "Can you call me back tomorrow?"

With her voice cracking, it sounded like she was starting to hyperventilate. "I was married to Kevin for only a year and your call has just opened up a lot of very painful wounds and memories."

"Oh, of course I can call back. I am so sorry. It was not my intent to do this to you. I am so sorry."

"Call tomorrow. I just need some time to think about this and see if I can talk about it. It was all so terrible."

"I understand, and I apologize for the pain I've caused you."

"OK."

Click.

* * * * *

Yikes! What had I done to the poor woman? Some stranger calls her out of the blue and wants to bring up a very painful part of her past. I felt terrible. So I waited several days before calling back.

"Hi, this is John Certalic again, I spoke to you a few days ago."

"Yes, I remember. I'm sorry I cut you off, but that period in my life was so awful. It was a very abusive marriage. But you asked about Kevin's father, Jack. He and Kevin were very similar. Angry, abusive men. Jack was very tall. His face was pock-marked, probably from acne as a kid years ago."

"Is he still alive?"

"I don't know. It's been many years since I last saw him."

"Do you know where he might be living now?"

"No."

"How about your ex-husband, Kevin? Do you know how I can reach him?"

"I don't have a phone number for him. The last I heard, he was living in Columbus, Ohio."

"Well, thank you so much. You've been very helpful to me. And again, I am sorry for reminding you of a painful part of your past."

"That's okay."

"Goodbye."

It was becoming clear to me that perhaps the path to Jack Byrd was through his son Kevin. But I called directory assistance in Columbus,

Ohio, and found no listing for him. What to do next? I went back to my notes and after looking through them, decided to re-contact Jack Byrd's ex-wives to see if they knew how I could reach the son, Kevin Byrd. I don't know why I hadn't thought of that before.

One of the ex-wives said, "Oh, Kevin. Yes, he is living in Columbus, Ohio now. I think I do have his phone number. Let me see, now. Where did I put it?"

Oh, please, dear God. Let her find the number.

"Yes, here it is. His phone number is …."

Now we were getting somewhere. Another lead, a good lead, to follow up. The adrenaline was flowing again. I now knew how to reach the closest relative yet to my birth father. But I was getting more nervous about blowing my cover. What if he was more inquisitive than all the others? What if he wanted to know how I thought I might be related to his father? I needed to be honest, yet I wanted to respect everyone's privacy. I didn't want a repeat of what had happened with the call to his ex-wife. It was getting a bit tense.

A week went by before I summoned the courage to call the son of my biological father. My half-brother, Kevin Byrd. Same father. Different mothers. It occurred to me then that all of my siblings are half-brothers or half-sisters—the four I grew up with, and the many others I had never met. Nothing in me seemed whole.

Everything was half. I was half-happy. Half-depressed. Nothing was full as it should be. I was not even fully adopted, for I had been raised by half of my birth parents, and adopted by the other half. This sometimes depressed me, too. If both my birth parents had abandoned me, maybe I would have had more reason to be depressed all the time as a kid and young adult.

Nothing was normal. That's how it felt during my search. Not long ago, though, I found some healing from this at a wedding for one of my nieces. I don't remember how we got on the subject but my brother Joe, who I grew up with, looked at one of my sisters and me, and shaking his head in disbelief, said, "I NEVER considered John my half-brother. He was always just my brother. Never just a half-brother." What wonderful healing words those were to me.

The search for my birth father, rather than depressing me, energized me. The next thing to do was to call his son, Kevin Byrd. After staring at the phone one evening, and picking it up and setting it down once or twice, I finally dialed his number.

"Hello, you don't know me, but my name is John Certalic. I'm doing some research into my family history and as part of this, I'm trying to locate a Jack Edward Byrd, and I understand you are his son. Am I correct?"

"Yes, I'm his son."

"Great. Is he still alive?"

"Yes, he is, last time I checked."

"Do you know where he is living now and how I can reach him?"

"Dad is living outside of Mobile, Alabama. He moved down there when he retired. He got tired of winters in the Midwest. I've got his phone number right here; I just talked to him a few days ago. Here's his number… Oh, and when you call, let the phone ring a long time. He's hard of hearing now and it will take him awhile to get to the phone."

"Thanks. I appreciate your help. Goodbye."

Now what?

* * * * *

I've talked to several other adoptees, read about others, and found varying views on locating one's birth parents. Some have no interest in finding theirs, feeling it would dishonor the parents who raised them. Others are consumed by it. I'm in the middle. I always had a curiosity about finding my birth father, and it nagged me at times, like a small pebble inside my shoe. At other times, it felt like a mill stone about to take me under.

I wouldn't call it a mid-life crisis; I did not feel driven to buy a red sports car. Tracking down of my birth father was different. It was about finding out who I am. It was about discovering my roots and where I had come from. It was about my identity.

The search for my roots was fresh on my mind when Janet and I got together with Brad and Kathy for another dinner date. Driving to the restaurant, I vowed I would not talk about what I was going through. It weighed so heavily on my heart that I needed a break from it all. We had gone out with them twice before, and both times when they asked how I was doing, I couldn't hold back the tears, for it started the playback of "I should never have been born." I didn't want to hear this song again, so I rehearsed in my mind that if they brought the subject up, I was going to stay calm and either say "I'd rather not talk about it," or just give some cursory facts to be polite.

It was a dark, wintry Saturday night when we pulled up to the restaurant. I dropped Janet off at the door, then drove down several rows of parked cars before I could find an empty stall for mine. When I walked in the door, I wasn't able to see Janet, nor Kathy and Brad, anywhere. They must have gotten a table already, I thought. So I began looking for them through the dim light. It took a while for my eyes to adjust, but I spotted them over in the corner at a round table. Table in the corner of a dark restaurant—good choice, I thought, given how I had been at the more recent times we've eaten out together. Besides faintly seeing their silhouettes through the dark light, I also spotted something else at the table. It would soon take my breath away.

As I neared the table, I could see tied to the empty chair they saved for me a yellow, helium-filled Mylar balloon emblazoned in very large letters, "He's here! It's a boy!" Just like the kind of balloon you find in a hospital gift shop you give to parents of newborns. It caught me so off-guard it took my breath away.

I sat down stunned. On my placemat was a card from Kathy and Brad, which on the front read "A baby is a gift of love—it's a boy. Congratulations!" And on the inside, they had written, "We are so happy you were born."

I stared at the card, still feeling the impact of the helium-filled balloon behind me. I couldn't speak. Nothing came out of me, except the tears I had committed to stuff down while in the parking lot just a few moments before. But these were different tears. Not tears of sorrow, as the others had been. But rather, tears of cleansing release, tears that washed away the dirt of my depression, tears that cleared my eyes so I could see what was true, what was real.

No one said anything. They just watched. Their long silence was so compassionate, so caring, so tender. All I could muster was "Thank you" and a huge sigh of relief. It seems odd now, but something very heavy lifted from me that night. It was like the helium in the balloon. Everything lightened from my heart and seemed to slowly float to the ceiling, through the roof, and gently through the cold night sky up to the stars that seemed to call it away. Far, far away, where it would no longer grip me as it had for so many years.

Several days later, I wrote a note to Brad and Kathy, which said in part,

> "I had a hard time sleeping Saturday night because I felt
> so loved. I felt in spite of how I came into the world that once
> I arrived, I was loved. I even felt close to my mother. It wasn't
> hard picturing her loving me. In the days since we met, I've
> thought about how God used you both to meet a very
> significant need in my life in helping me over a tough
> obstacle. I've thought about how much God loves you, Brad,
> and how much God loves you, Kathy, to use you in such a
> wonderful and mysterious way to bless me. In praying to God,
> I've also thought how much he loved me in sending both of

you into my life, and how much he loved me to let me experience the profound sense of belonging and cared-for-ness last Saturday night.

I just know what you did was from God and I'm so grateful you were sensitive to his leading. I wish I could explain why, but what you did is a real turning point in my life. I knew at that moment when I saw "It's a boy! Congratulations!" that I was loved, that it was right that I was born and that I was born on purpose for a purpose—and that I didn't really have to deal with this issue anymore—that it was settled.

While I feel so loved and blessed by you, and so loved and blessed by God, I really want to follow through and be a blessing to others, like you were to me. I'd like to help people draw closer to Jesus like you have done with me. Because ultimately, when you come right down to it, the real measure of a friend is how they draw us closer to Jesus. And the two of you have measured up spectacularly well. I hope someday I can do the same for you."

I ended the note by mentioning that through them, I gained a glimpse of what Ephesians 3:17-19 is all about.

"And I pray that you, being rooted and established in love, may have power together with all the saints, to grasp how wide and long and high and deep is the love of Christ, and to know this love that surpasses knowledge—that you may be filled to the measure of all the fullness of God."

* * * * *

After about a month of sitting on the phone number of my birth father, and rehearsing what I would say to him when we talked, I finally summoned up the nerve to make the call. Part of my delay in calling, I realized later, was that the search for him was what energized me, not the actual contact with him. The adrenaline rush was over.

I had no illusions that he would respond well when I called. I don't even know what responding well would have looked like. I mean, the man had married seven times. There was no thinking in my mind that he would rejoice at my call, sob uncontrollably, and once he composed himself would say something like, "Oh, I've wondered about you and thought about you most every day since I first heard you were going to be born. Your mother would not return my phone calls. I even stopped at her apartment on one of my trips, but no one was home. I wrote to her a number of times, but she never wrote back. Then I lost track of her. I am SO glad you called, and I do hope you can find it in your heart to forgive me for not being able to support you when you were a child. If you have it your heart to forgive me, I really would like to see you face to face."

A more realistic response, I thought, would be his denial that he was my birth father. He might even hang up on me. I'd be fine with either. The court records told me all I needed to know about his character.

"Hello, is this Jack Byrd?

"Yes, it is."

"My name is John Certalic, and I'm doing some family history work and I think you and I might be related."

"Really?"

"Yes, does the name Renee Morris ring a bell with you?"

"No, can't say as it does."

"You would have met her in the late 1940s when you were a truck driver and used to make runs to Milwaukee where she lived. She was from northern Minnesota and worked for the telephone company."

"Hmmn. This does sound familiar, now that you say it."

"Well, I am her son, and she tells me you are my father."

Long silence. Dead air. Nothing. What is he going to say now? What came out of his mouth surprised me.

"Well, well," with a jovial laugh as would come from a gentle grandfather, "I guess I have children all over the country I didn't even know about."

We talked for a bit more, exchanged addresses, and agreed to send pictures of each other.

Neither of us ever did.

* * * * *

We continued to remain friends—Janet, Kathy, Brad and me. Janet, of course, knew all about my conversation with Jack Byrd, and when I told Brad and Kathy, they listened well and were very supportive. No tears or emotion came, for they were all purged the night they gave me the balloon and the "Congratulations-we're-so-glad-you-were-born" card. Our friendship continued, but when we started attending different churches, we drifted apart and didn't see each other anymore. But what they did that night with a helium-filled balloon and a simple card came in handy as a sermon illustration fifteen years later.

For some reason I still don't understand, I was asked to preach a four-part series on caring for others at a church we had recently started attending. The first sermon was to be about one of my favorite stories in the Bible from the Gospel of Mark where Jesus cared for some difficult people in his life—his own disciples.

I like that story because the disciples remind me of how difficult a person I was for the people in my life during the search for my birth father. The disciples didn't create a scene in a restaurant like I did, but they certainly needed help when Jesus told them to row across the Sea of Galilee soon after He had fed 5,000 men and their families. Maybe it was the food; I don't know. In both my story and the disciples' story, food brought out the worst in us—and the best in the people who cared for us.

When the disciples did what Jesus told them by getting into the boat on the large lake that is the Sea of Galilee, a storm came up. It caused them to strain at the oars to make it to the other side. They were obedient, yet as the Gospel writer Mark tells us, they were struggling, they were fearful, and their hearts were hardened toward Jesus. The thing that gets them out of their predicament was Jesus walking from shore onto the water to meet them and get in the boat with them. He says very little in doing so, but in getting in the boat with the obedient, but scared and hardened men, Jesus makes their problem go away. The winds die down and the seas calm, all because Jesus gets in the boat with them.

As I prepared this sermon, I was reminded how years earlier my friends Brad and Kathy, did what Jesus did. They got in the boat with me, didn't say much, but listened and cared for me by just being there. Their presence, even when I made several scenes in several restaurants, calmed the stormy seas in my life, just as Jesus getting in the boat with His frightened, hardhearted apostles calmed the Sea of Galilee and their hearts as well.

Jesus, Brad, and Kathy illustrate the principle that we tend to overestimate the power of words, but underestimate the power of our presence. We think we need to say something, that we need to dispense wise, comforting, and helpful words to care for people. But on days when we're not feeling terribly wise because we've misplaced the car keys or can't figure out how to program our DVR, we feel so inadequate.

Most of caring is just showing up, but it is so hard to do when our own needs and inadequacies nag at us like dirty dishes in the sink crying for our attention. Caring for others exposes our perceived shortcomings of who we are and what we're capable of. *What if I say the wrong thing? What if I make things worse? What if I can't fix this person's problem? What will all of this say about ME?*

I planned to mention in my sermon that caring for others is not about us. It's about them. It's about being available to God to be used to draw people to His son Jesus. It's not about being a competent problem-solver or wise advice-giver. It's about reflecting the image of God well and being His representative. It's about getting out of the way so the Holy Spirit can work in someone's heart without interference from us.

That's what Kathy and Brad did for me that night, and this is what we can all do for each other. In my better moments, as rare as they are, I find myself asking the question of myself. I wonder if there's someone God is asking me to get into the boat with. Not conventional grammar, I know. But sometimes the best thoughts have the worst English.

So that's what I prepared to talk about in my sermon that Sunday morning. Moments before the service began, I was stunned to see two people seated in the audience I had not seen or talked to in years—Brad and Kathy.

Chapter 5

The Visitor No One Wants

Depression on my left, Loneliness on my right.
They don't need to show me their badges.
I know these guys very well.
— Elizabeth Gilbert

Nine months passed after I spoke to Jack Byrd. No communication to him or from him. It didn't matter because I got what I wanted out of my search for him. I learned more about where I came from, which fortunately I've come to appreciate does not determine where I am going.

Understanding where I have come from is helpful in dealing with the present, for many of my current dysfunctions have their roots in the past. The better I understand this, the less control my history has in how I think and behave. I don't want to be controlled by my past, yet sometimes it grips me, like a demanding toddler pulling at my pants leg to get my attention. It is easy for me to see this in other people, and so difficult to see it in myself.

It's sad to see some people controlled by their past, where they try to make up for deficiencies from an earlier time by how they live in the present, thinking it will change the past. It often comes out as trying to prove something to someone, like a grown man trying to prove to his dad he has what it takes to make it in life. Showing he can compete with other men and come out on top, to make up for all the times he disappointed his father as a ten-year-old when he struck out with the bases loaded in Little League.

There are grown women trying to please their aging mothers, because deep down in their hearts there's a little bird chirping away, "Maybe if you do everything you can to please your mom, she'll finally give you the love you needed when you were six. It will be forty years late, but it's better than nothing. So keep on working to earn her love."

I say wring that little birdie's neck and bury it in the backyard, because what the little bird is telling you just isn't going to happen. Face the reality that Mom isn't going to change. I mean, she's eighty-four and she hasn't changed yet, so what makes you think she'll change now? Is there ever going to be a time when you've done enough for her? Face it, no matter what you do, it's never going to be enough.

To come to grips with a mom like that is to face the sadness of knowing she's never going to be the mother you need and deserve. Yet you can and should love a mother like that. Do what you can to make sure she has food, clothing, and shelter. Honor her, and respect her choices, even the one where she chooses to live a very self-centered life. But don't give her the power to determine your happiness.

I know it is easier said than done. Sometimes, it really is easier to be depressed over not getting what we needed from our parents—then and now. I grew up being depressed. As an adult, I've gone through periods of depression—never enough to require medication, but just feeling down a lot. After finding Jack Byrd, however, and Kathy and Brad getting into my boat during that time, my periods of depression have been shorter, with longer times in-between. Even my birthday in February, which was always very troublesome, usually seems to pass now with minimal reflection on how I came into the world.

I don't think the church knows what to do with us depressed types. Janet and I were once in a church where the pastor preached from the pulpit warnings to beware of our own "pity parties." It made me cringe when he said that. It marginalized all of us who were depressed, which just made things worse. By implication, we were all to just stop feeling depressed. *Just stop it. Think and will your way out of your depression and you'll be fine.* It doesn't work that way. He was an extrovert, and as nice of a man as he was, he didn't understand depressed people. He seemed to view depression as something we just needed to try harder to get over.

I wonder who he modeled himself after as a pastor. Maybe he saw himself following in the footsteps of pastors who came from the "People Need to Be Corrected" boot camp. I hear they have a training center in the remote Arizona desert. That particular pastor often talked about the biblical imagery of people as sheep. The ignorance and stupidity of sheep came up frequently in his sermons.

I prefer pastors from the "People Need to be Wooed to Jesus" camp. Their training takes place on a Caribbean cruise ship in January.

To my mind, the best pastors have spent time in both camps. The best ones are often those who started in the "People Need to Be Corrected" boot camp, but who eventually end up on the "People Need to be Wooed to Jesus" cruise ship.

Another thing the church doesn't understand about all of us depressed people shows up when it sings the "Just Join a Small Group and All Your Problems Will Go Away" hymn. I recently heard a pastor say that to become a member of his church, you *HAVE TO* join a small group. Now who could possibly say anything negative about small groups? I mean, some churches even have small group pastors, for heaven's sake. I know, I know, small groups are very helpful. Jesus spent the last three years of his life pouring himself into his small group of twelve apostles. So without minimizing the value of small groups, how about acknowledging they aren't for everyone during every season of life?

Sometimes, when I'm feeling depressed, I wish for just one person to listen to me, to show a little compassion. Knowing that another person understands what I'm going through often is really enough to help me move on.

For a brief time, I went to see Marilyn for my depression. I paid her, because it was her job—she was a counselor in private practice. She was also a professor of mine in grad school where I learned to be a counselor myself. I liked her style in the classroom, and we got along well. But I had to pay her when I went to see her for counseling. She deserved every cent. Most therapists do. In fact, I think they're underpaid for the impact they have in people's lives. But you'll never see a protest movement or picket line supporting underpaid counselors. But if there was one, I'd join in. There's still a part of the late '60s in me.

A forty-something friend of mine told me on one occasion how much counseling had helped him when he was in his mid-twenties. This came up in the context of talking about his twin brother, who chose not to go for counseling over some father issues they both had.

"Andy has been an angry man all his life. He blames Dad for much that is wrong in his life. When Dad died two years ago, I was really at peace with my relationship with him. Andy wasn't, and isn't. I had some issues with Dad, too, but one day I was sitting in a park, thinking about what I was learning in counseling, and suddenly, just like that, the skies opened up for me and I could see Dad in a new light. I realized he loved me, but spoke a different love language than I do. I needed to be loved with words, but he loved me by spending time with me. I got the love, just in a different form. What a freeing realization that was. And it changed my whole view of God. I could now see God as a loving God, someone I could approach.

"Andy has never gotten to that place. He's still bitter over not getting the love in the form he wanted."

I love this story.

I love it because it shows the value of counseling, and the benefit of going through it earlier rather than later. I'm so glad for my forty-something friend, but sad for his twin brother carrying all that anger and bitterness around with him for so long, like a bowling ball chained to his heart.

This story also grabs me because it achieved the most important goal of Christian counseling—helping people draw closer to God. What a great privilege and honor it is to work with people to help them get rid of the emotional and spiritual junk in their lives that interferes with their relationship with God. We can do the same thing with each other as friends, but all too often, we're so busy with our own little lives that we miss the great joy in caring for others.

I heard someone say that in church work, the better the preaching, the less need there will be for counseling. I believe this. I also believe the better the quality of our friendships, the less need there will be for counseling. And the better all of us listened to each other, the less need we'd have for therapy.

As good as Marilyn was, I still had to pay her. Did I mention that yet? But Marilyn and my other therapist friends don't have to worry about going out of business. Preaching that fails to touch the heart, along with dysfunctional relationships, and our poor listening skills, will keep counselors in business for a long, long time.

One thing I learned from Marilyn is that depression can actually be a good thing—for a short time. It forces you to slow down, to think and reflect. Yeah, I like this. Thinking and reflecting are good. I know for some people, depression has a physical component to it. Lack of certain chemicals in the brain. Anti-depressants replenish those chemicals, and while they don't change how you think and respond, they do make it easier to process what is really happening.

My own depression wasn't a physical issue, as much as it was a thinking problem. Emotions not organically based come from our reactions to things. My depression is my response to stuff that happens. I often can't change what happens, but I can change my reaction to events by reframing my experience in a way that more accurately portrays what is true. Sometimes, things in life are simply sad, and no amount of right-thinking is going to change that, so we just have to sit in the sadness. How we deal with our sadness is another subject altogether, one I haven't quite figured out yet.

I can feel depressed, really depressed, for a few days and then something out of the blue will happen and the depression lifts, just like that. The energy returns. Often over something totally unrelated to what brought on the depression in the first place. Kind of like what happened with my wife and her mother not too long ago.

Elda is a 93-year-old widow with dementia who lives in an assisted living memory care facility. On a recent visit, Elda told Janet, "I don't know why I am still alive. All the people I knew are dead. There's no reason for me to live."

Janet just listened, paused and then said, "You know, Mom, I need you. You're my mother and I still need you, no matter how old you are."

Elda listened, then asked for the fourth time in ten minutes, "Where am I living now?" After Janet answered for the fourth time in ten minutes, she said, "Say, Mom, why don't we get in the car and go get an ice cream cone?"

"Okay," Elda said with a smile. "Now where is my jacket?"

With that, Elda's depression lifted, and off they went for an ice cream cone and a pleasant afternoon together. What a beautiful thing Janet did for her mother. She set aside her own frustration at having to continually repeat herself, and the ongoing grief of seeing her mother descend the spiral staircase of dementia. Janet thought of what could she do to make things a little better for her mother. Maybe it was the thought of ice cream that brought Elda back to life. I don't know. Just as something will trigger the onset of depression, sometimes something else will trigger a response that gets us out of it. It's how it works at times with depression. At least for Elda and me.

Besides slowing a person down, which can lead to some important quality think-time, there's another advantage to depression. It makes us sensitive to other depressed people, if we let it. Depression at times will visit me like an uninvited relative from another state who shows up unexpectedly on my doorstep late in the afternoon.

"Surprise! I'm back again. Don't know how long I'll stay this time, but if you'll kindly get out of the doorway, I'll bring my bags in and go to my room. So glad I've been here before; I know just where everything is. Oh, and don't mind me. Just go about your business and I'll just follow you around wherever you go. Won't this be fun?"

It isn't.

Depression stays a few days and follows me around, pointing out how all the glasses in my life are half-empty. Then Depression helps me notice other depressed people. Like waitresses in restaurants. I learn from Depression how to read people's eyes and their countenances. Depression teaches me to find meaning between the lines of what people say, and to notice the important words they don't speak. From that, I begin to develop a measure of compassion for people, which frees me from my half-empty-glass life.

Then as suddenly as Depression arrived, he leaves. I almost want to thank him for heightening my sensitivity to other people. For making me more aware of the needs of others. Most of the year I was actively searching for my birth father, I was often pretty clueless as to the needs of others. I was so wrapped up in the pain in my own life, I couldn't see the pain in the lives of other people. After tracking him down, and then my telephone conversation with Jack Edward Byrd, I was able to put things to rest more easily. That all changed about six months later when the telephone rang one sunny Sunday autumn afternoon.

"Hello."

"Hello. Is this John Certalic?"

"Yes, it is."

"You don't know me, but my name is Judy Capes."

I went silent for what seemed like an hour as I processed what I just heard and speculated what it might mean. Why was she calling? How did she find me? Was I going to be in trouble? All these thoughts raced through my head, like an auctioneer's rapid review of bids for used farm equipment at a foreclosure.

What did I do wrong now? was the question that always popped into my mind at times like this. The answer was almost always nothing, but growing up as a kid, I always assumed I was doing something wrong. What other explanation could there be for my mother yelling and slapping me in the face so many times?

"You don't know me, but my name is Judy Capes."

But I did know something of Judy Capes.

She is Jack Byrd's first child from his first of six marriages. I learned about her from court records I had found in Fort Wayne. From phone calls to family connections of Jack Byrd, I also discovered she at one time owned a dress shop for tall women in Marion, Indiana.

She continued. "I was talking to Dad recently and he told me about your call to him several months ago. He wrote you a card and sent a few pictures, but they came back to him in the mail. Apparently you moved and the forwarding address expired."

She was right. I had given him my office address rather than my home address, and I had moved my business to another part of town before he wrote to me. I was surprised it had been that long since I talked to him.

"Dad asked if I would try to track you down for him. So I just searched online and found you rather easily."

"I see."

"I guess you and I are brother and sister then," she gracefully remarked, trying to end the awkward silence.

"I guess so."

So Judy knew.

In my search for Jack Edward Byrd, I didn't want to open up a can of worms for him or his other children or ex-wives. So I never tipped my hand to share with any of them that I was his illegitimate child, the one he kept secret from everyone.

"Tell me about yourself, then. And how did you find Dad?"

Now that she knew, I had no reason to be secretive, so I gave her a quick summary of my life and told her how I found the man she called "Dad," but for whom I had no title other than the antiseptic, "Birth father."

"So that's me, Judy. Tell me about you."

I learned she was living in Leesburg, Indiana—just twenty minutes from our daughter's in-laws, a couple with whom we became friends when our kids married.

Among other things, I learned Judy had indeed owned a women's dress shop, but spent most of her working life as a human resources manager at a local manufacturing company. She was divorced with several adult children and lived with Jim, a wonderful man who cares for her, very much unlike her father, Jack E. Byrd.

We had a long talk, a very pleasant one that concluded with Judy saying, "I'd like to meet you in person. Any chance we could do that when you visit your daughter's in-laws?"

"Possibly," I said. "We don't get down to Indiana as much anymore now that our daughter has moved back to Milwaukee. But I would like to see you, too."

Shortly thereafter, the conversation ended. I thought, *Do I have room for another relationship?*

Within six months, Janet and I were visiting Judy. Meeting her renewed my curiosity about Jack Edward Byrd, the one person we had in common.

The Saturday afternoon of our meeting, Janet and I drove up the gravel road to where Judy lived in semi-rural Leesburg, Indiana. We turned a bend in the fire lane that separated two rows of one-story homes on small lots in between two channels of a lake we later learned was good for fishing. Within a minute of pulling up to her tasteful and well-maintained yellow home, she came out to greet us as we got out of our car.

She's very tall, just like me, was my first thought. Just like her father, as described to me by his former daughter-in-law.

"She looks like you. I could see the resemblance right away," Janet would tell me later.

As we got out of the car, Judy walked over to us, welcomed us, and gave me a big hug.

My eyes began tearing up, as they do so embarrassingly often.

* * * * *

Judy's partner, Jim, introduced himself, and after some small talk, he left to run some errands. I liked him right away. I spent the next several hours asking Judy questions to fill in the blanks, the holes in my research about who was related to whom and information about each of our siblings, and Jack Byrd's ex-wives. I also asked lots of questions about her father, who was my I-don't-know-what. She told me that during WWII, he had been in the Army and served as a railroad worker in Italy. Judy had only lived with him the first year of her life in 1940, then was sent to live with his parents because her father and mother didn't have the means to raise a child. This was quite painful for her to talk about.

I learned how Jack Byrd had abandoned her, too, and how she pursued him many times, only to be ignored or stood up when she arranged meetings in local restaurants. She described the times she and

Jim would visit him in Florida, and how cruel and abusive he would be to waitresses in restaurants. It was all so painful for her to recall and share with me. It moved me to hear her share the wounds in her heart over her upbringing, and then her marriage, which had ended in divorce.

Her pain connected us. She had emotional holes in her heart like I did. She showed me family pictures of Jack Edward Byrd and his relatives. One stood out in particular. It was taken several years after the war, before he met my mother. It was of him walking down a street in New York City holding a cigarette in one hand, dressed in a sport coat and open-collared shirt, looking a bit like a young Dean Martin. Maybe he had picked up that cocky, carefree look during his time in Italy. I pictured him with my mother. Charming her, preying on her rural Minnesota farm-girl personality.

The hours passed like minutes before we had to leave. We both promised to stay in touch with each other, which we have done. A year or so later, Judy and Jim came to visit us for a few days in Milwaukee. Knowing they're both avid Chicago Cubs fans, we took them to a Milwaukee Brewers game when the Cubs were in town. We all enjoyed it immensely, especially Jim.

Prior to the game starting, and while sitting in our seats near the Cubs' dugout, Jim called several of his friends on his cell phone, "You'll never guess where I am! You'll never guess!"

Months passed and one day I got an e-mail from Judy, saying she was going to arrange a family reunion at her house some Sunday afternoon in the fall.

"I do hope you and Janet can come. We are flying Dad up, and Jim and I are going to drive down to the Indianapolis airport to pick him up the Saturday before. He doesn't know anything about this, and I'm not going to tell him until he gets off the plane. If I told him now, he probably wouldn't come. So that's why I'm going to spring it on him once he's off the plane. There's a distinct possibility, though, he might turn around and fly right back home to Florida. I'm willing to take the risk, though."

Judy continued. "I've already talked to my other brothers and sisters, and all except one plan to come. Some of them have not seen or talked to Dad in over thirty years. I sure hope you can come."

That call set the stage for the most awkward afternoon I have ever spent in my life.

Chapter 6

What Could Have Been, But Never Was

I don't know half of you half as well as I should like;
and I like less than half of you half as well as you deserve.
—J.R.R. Tolkien

J anet and I were the last of the children to arrive at this most unusual of family reunions. Judy greeted us as we got out of the car and graciously introduced us to her other brothers and sisters. My half brothers and sisters, and hers, too. We had all come from the same father, but from a multitude of mothers. Everyone was polite and cordial, but either guarded or terribly shy. I fit right in with them.

Knowing they knew who I was helped. I imagined them thinking "Oh, yeah, Dad's illegitimate son from Milwaukee he never told us about. I wonder if he brought any beer or cheese?" But then I remembered what Janet says, "People are thinking a whole lot less about you than you think they are."

No one asked me any questions at that point, but people rarely do. I ask people questions about themselves all the time, mostly because I'm genuinely interested in other people and often find them fascinating, but sometimes I ask questions to keep people at bay. If I ask the right questions and get people talking about themselves, they won't ask me anything. If they do ask questions of me, they usually don't inquire beyond the surface of my responses. Or they use what I answer as a springboard to return the conversation to talking about themselves. It's disappointing when this happens, when no one asks follow-up questions, when no one asks about my feelings, or how I process the day-to-day events of my life. I understand, because I do this to people, too. So to avoid the disappointment, I deflect people's surface inquiry into my life by shifting the focus back onto them.

What appears as shyness or even aloofness to people is most often my self-protective defenses kicking in. I don't want to be hurt by sharing a part of who I am, and then have that part ignored or discounted. It's just safer not to share much that's deep inside. Pretty dysfunctional, I know.

At church recently, a friend remarked to me, "You seem very quiet today."

"I have nothing to say, I guess."

"I don't have that problem," he replied. "I always have something to say. But I need to be a better listener."

"That's a very worthwhile goal," I said in my effort to encourage him.

I don't know when it happened, but a long time ago, I decided I wasn't going to fight for airtime in conversations with people. It isn't worth it. You lose a lot more than you gain. You lose by fighting for the talking team, rather than the listening team. The talking team has thousands of players on its side. The listening team? Very few. I like rooting for the underdog, and the listening team is arguably the most underdog of all underdogs. There's a part of me that's always been a little contrarian, and being on the listening team is about as contrarian as you can get. It fits me well.

As we sat in Judy's living room, I talked a little, but mostly listened and drew people out to learn about them. They comprised an interesting group, and I was enjoying myself. Then the door bell rang, the front door opened, and in walked a tall, slightly hunched over, silver-haired old man.

It was Jack Edward Byrd.

Wearing a white and peach-colored Ban-Lon sport shirt, gray polyester pants, and white shoes, my birth father looked every bit the part of an eighty-year-old retiree from Florida.

"Hi, everyone," he announced to those in the living room. He straightened his shoulders and began walking around the room, extending his handshake to some. He walked past me with a fleeting "Hello." What a terribly awkward moment.

While he had never met me before, I learned later he had not seen or had contact with some of his other children in over thirty years. He seemed like the next door neighbor who just stopped over to borrow a plumber's snake to clean out a clogged drain.

I watched him engage with the others in small talk. He appeared comfortable, while most of the rest of us looked ill at ease. It was a meeting of strangers. Judy later told me some of her siblings, who live within forty miles of each other, had not seen or talked to each other since high school. Though I dislike ice-breakers, I felt like we needed one at that moment. Something like, *"Share with your partner a favorite childhood memory."*

It was an afternoon of small talk around a really big elephant in the room—Jack E. Byrd, the father of us all. I had no illusions the afternoon would later be reenacted in a Hallmark made-for-TV movie. But I did have one *What if?* scenario go through my mind that would be quite remarkable if it actually occurred. There would be a moment of silence, at which point Jack Byrd would announce to the group, "Say everyone, it's a bit crowded here in the house and it's so nice outside this beautiful October afternoon, can we all meet in the backyard? There is something I want to say to everyone."

In my *What if?* dream, I imagine we all glance at each other with surprised looks on our faces as we move to the backyard, and listen to Jack Byrd begin,

"First of all, I want to thank Judy for arranging this reunion, and for her and Jim flying me up here for this get-together. They took a big risk, not knowing how I'd respond. And I must admit, when they told me at the Indianapolis airport what they cooked up, the thought of turning around and heading back to Florida did cross my mind. My reluctance in seeing all of you had nothing to do with you; it's all about me and the regret and shame I feel for the unique pain I've caused each of you. For the unwanted baggage each of you are carrying around because of my failure as your father.

"Life is hard enough, and fathers should be there to make it easier for their children, not harder, as I have. And for this I am terribly, terribly sorry. I am so sorry and regret so much the role I've played in your lives, and for the role I didn't play. I abandoned each of your mothers. When I left them, that too was all about me. I didn't treat them well either. It never occurred to me that by leaving each of your mothers, I was leaving you, too. I was so selfish, so self-centered that I couldn't see beyond my own needs to ever consider yours. You didn't deserve that. You deserved much more than you received from me.

"I modeled for you what it means to break vows, wedding vows. I modeled for you what lack of commitment looks like. I taught you by my example that people are there to be used, to meet our needs, rather than as opportunities for us to pour our lives into others to bring out the best in them. I am so sorry for all of this. I have failed you greatly.

"Judy, I am so sorry that when you were a little girl just one year old, I took you to live with my parents to be raised by them, rather than doing it myself with your mother. Times were hard economically, but it is just an excuse. A cop-out on my part. I lacked the character needed in a father, and you saw this played out many times from then on. As an adult, you went out of your way to pursue me. You set up lunch meetings with me that I so often failed to keep. You and Jim went out of your way to visit me in Florida, only to be met with criticism and orneriness on my part. So many times, I embarrassed you in restaurants with my rude behavior with waitresses. I am so sorry and am embarrassed at myself.

"And John. What can I say to you? You were a secret I kept for so many years. No one knew about you. I wish I could say I thought of you often and longed to know what happened to you. But I didn't. I am so sorry for the predicament I put you and your mother in because of my reckless and irresponsible behavior. I took advantage of your mother behind my wife's back at the time. She was an innocent, naive farm girl from northern Minnesota and I used that to my advantage to satisfy my own pleasure. I hope your real father, the man who raised you and sacrificed for you, gave you what you needed. From what I can tell today, it looks like he did. When you see your mother, please tell her how sorry I am for the pain I caused her so many years ago. The only positive thing that came out of this was that you were born, and hopefully, you are making a positive difference in the lives of others in ways I haven't.

"So everyone, I know it's really, really late for this, but I would like to get to know all of you all over again. I'd like to start having a positive impact in your life. And I'd like to start right now. I'm not sure what it will look like, but I would like to give it try.

"Thank you for coming, and thank you for listening."

I knew this *What if?* fantasy would most likely not happen. And it didn't. Not by a long shot. Hallmark will have to look elsewhere for its next script. But it is how it should have been. It would have been the right thing to do. Even if the right thing doesn't happen. Even if what ought to happen doesn't, how are we to live? For me, it comes down to understanding the dynamics of goals and desires.

Goals and Desires

Finally meeting Jack E. Byrd reminded me of a really helpful concept I picked up at a conference years ago. It's about the difference between goals and desires. It was Larry Crabb who explained it, more as an afterthought to something else he was talking about. For me, it has become more of a forethought that has helped me a great deal. It goes like this:

A *goal* is something I alone have control over, whether I achieve it or not. It is something I can work toward, and if I work hard and smart, I can achieve it. A goal is something that depends on me and my efforts and skills. Losing weight is an example. It's something I have control over. It's not rocket science. If I choose to eat less food and consume fewer calories, I will lose weight. If I add exercise to consuming fewer calories, I'll lose a little more weight. There may be genetic and environmental conditions that make losing weight more difficult, but it can be done. It is a goal I can achieve by the decisions I make and the behaviors I choose. It's up to me and no one else. Achieving a goal depends upon me working to accomplish it.

Desires are something else. A desire is something I want, and may even work toward, but fulfilling it depends upon people or forces over which I have no control. Wanting our young-adult children to make it in life, to have successful careers and satisfying relationships, is a worthy desire, but ultimately, not something we have any degree of control over. I can work on my relationship with them certainly, but as much as I want the best for a single twenty-seven-year-old son who can't hold down a job, it's really up to him. I have control over myself, over my behaviors and choices, but I don't have control over others, their limitations, and what they choose to do. Because desires depend on someone or something I have no control over, the best we can do to fulfill our desires is to pray for them. Pray? Yes, pray.

Work toward goals. Pray for desires.

Where I get into trouble sometimes is because I do just the opposite. I pray for goals, and work for desires.

I think we should pray about lots and lots of things, but many times, more than prayer is required. We need to act. We need to do something. If my goal is to move out of my tiny two-bedroom apartment with my dog and cat and buy a condo, I can pray all I want, but if I don't have enough money for a down payment, and if I don't earn enough to pay the monthly mortgage, my goal will never be achieved. I have control over how much money I save, and even how much money I earn. I may need to switch jobs or careers, move to another state, go back to school to acquire more marketable skills so I can earn and save more. It's something I have control over. There are choices I can make to achieve my goals. We all have more choices than we think.

I notice sometimes when people feel trapped in life, it's often because they feel they don't have choices, when in fact they do. It's just that the consequences of those choices may not be very appealing. Switch jobs? Well, then I couldn't be on the softball team at work (honestly, someone once told me this as the reason he didn't want to leave a job he hated. You can't make this stuff up. Horrible job, but a great softball team. Go figure.)

Go back to school? Yeah, but I'd be going to class one to two nights a week, not to mention all the studying and giving up my weekends to write papers and cram for exams. *It's a choice.*

Save more money? But I really like going out to eat two or three times a week, and I could never give up cable—there's so much junk on the major networks. *It's a choice.*

Give up my dog and cat? Lulu and Mr. T are a part of me. My condo association is really being unreasonable. *It's a choice.*

All of these choices are things we have control over. We may not like the consequences of those choices, but they're choices nevertheless.

Several years ago, Dave, a friend of mine, wanted to spend more time with his family. He was a pilot with a major airline, and because he was lower on the seniority list than most, he got stuck with flying on weekends and holidays. His family missed him during important family events, and he certainly missed them. So he approached his company to ask for a leave of absence to take time to figure out what could be done to solve his family problem. The airline denied his request. His wife is a physician, and after months of thinking it over, he resigned and walked away from his career as an airline pilot. It was really hard for him, as his identity was tied up in being a pilot. But to achieve the goal he wanted, he made the difficult choice to become a stay-at-home-dad, while his wife worked in her medical practice. He certainly prayed about the decision, but he worked to make his goal happen—he quit a job he really liked.

I know people who only pray about things and never take any action on their own. They pray their employer will suddenly break a union contract, as the airline would have had to do for my friend, Dave. They pray the company would grant them a benefit they wouldn't grant to thousands of other employees. Yeah, right. It's not going to happen.

Dave had a goal, and he worked to achieve it. He was in control, and no one else.

Then there is the matter of desires.

The October afternoon I met my birth father for the first time, I wanted to see in-person who I had come from as the child of an unwed mother. I knew my mother, but I wanted to know more about the other variable in the equation that produced me. I wanted to see up close the source of my thinking I should never have been born.

Had that October afternoon happened thirty years prior, my desire would have been entirely different. In those days, I longed to be understood. If people understood me, so my subconscious reasoning went, they would probably like me, and if they liked me, they would most likely care about me, and even care for me. I would have wanted to meet Jack E. Byrd in the flesh for him to know me and to understand what this baggage of being an illegitimate child has done to me. Because if he really understood me and what I've been through, he just might say or do something to make the pain go away. This would have been my thinking and my desire. Fortunately, I didn't meet him thirty years ago. I was not ready.

All of this was my desire. It was something I had no control over, for it all would depend on him and how he responded to me. If we had met back then, I'm pretty sure I would have treated my desire as a goal, and worked at achieving it. I would have taken him aside and confronted him with all that I experienced because of him. I would have been cordial, yet to the point, explaining what it was like to never feel like I fit in. I would have told him how the time around my birthday each February was the most depressing time of the year for me. Lots of "I statements," just like they talk about in *Therapy for Dummies*. For surely if I confronted him, the scales would fall from his eyes and heart, Tchaikovsky's *1812 Overture* would blast in the background, and he would see the error of his ways and beg for my forgiveness. If only he understood. If only he understood.

I would have worked really hard at trying to fulfill my desire because I didn't understand at the time that I had no control over whether my birth father, or anyone else for that matter, liked me, wanted a relationship with me, or cared about me. I wasted a lot of energy in those days trying to make people understand me. If they were upset at me about something I did or said, it was because they just didn't understand. It surely couldn't be they were right about my flawed behavior. No, no, no.

In more recent years, I've learned while there's nothing wrong with desiring people to like me and care about me, it's not something I should work toward. Behave myself, help old ladies across the street, and so on. Sure, I have control over that. But I don't have control over how others relate to me. Instead, I need to pray others respond to me in the way I would like.

In meeting Jack E. Byrd for the first time, I had my goals and desires in their proper place. I had no expectations anything good would come from the encounter other than satisfaction in understanding more about who I have come from. Besides meeting my biological father that afternoon, I also met my half brothers and sisters. One brother stood out in particular.

While we were outside, he took me aside, and in a confrontational manner very close to my face, asked, "Judy has told us about you. Why are you here? What do you want? Are you after the money when Dad dies?"

He was suspicious and a bit angry. One thing I've learned about angry people is often their anger comes from fear. Seems like this was a monetary fear for him. If I get a slice of the $48.90 estate, his piece would be smaller. *The money after Dad dies?* The thought never occurred to me. Maybe he knew more than I did, but it didn't seem to me there was any money to be had.

Hmm, I thought. *He doesn't understand me and my need to know where I've come from.* Knowing where we have all come from can give us a greater appreciation of where we are in life now. Unless of course, we grew up in a Fifth Avenue apartment across from New York City's Central Park, but now live in a van down by the river.

I told him, "No, the reason I'm here is I simply want to know more about where I've come from—to learn more about my origin. That's all. Nothing more. Honest."

This seemed to calm him down. He backed away. I told Judy about it later and she just rolled her eyes. "That's Kevin," she said.

While it was the most awkward afternoon of my life, I was glad I came to see Jack E. Byrd. There was no one-on-one interaction with him. And I felt no need to talk to him, to ask him any questions, though I probably should have asked about his health history, but Judy had filled me in earlier. Doctors and insurance companies want to know more about my genetics than I do, though I must admit I wonder where my predisposition to chapped lips comes from. Maybe that is the legacy he handed down to me.

The adrenaline rush I felt over my six-month investigative search was long past. I found what I needed to know. My goal was met, but not my desire. And that was okay. Really. It would have been wonderful if he had reached out to me, sought forgiveness, and affirmed me. But he didn't. He was incapable of it. In praying about this desire, I learned how I came into the world doesn't really matter. It's what happens afterwards that counts.

Several years after meeting Jack E. Byrd, Judy invited me to a follow-up reunion. I thought about going, but I didn't need to any longer. I got what I needed the first time around. Then, several years after that, I got an e-mail from Judy that Jack E. Byrd had died. The funeral service was going to be in Florida, just fifty miles from where I was facilitating a conference for missionaries. I felt no need to go for me, but really wanted to for Judy's sake. To get in the boat with her, to support her, but the timing didn't work out and I couldn't go, given my responsibilities at the conference.

Judy was so kind and caring of me; I wish I could have been that for her. She cared well for me from the day she contacted me out of the blue on behalf of Jack Byrd. She invited me to her home to connect with me, and to fill in the gaps I had about where I had come from. It was through her that God brought a great deal of healing in my life.

I was at peace by this time with my relationship with my birth father, largely because I came to have peace about my dysfunctional, disturbing childhood. He was just the embodiment of all that went wrong in my growing-up years. My desire to have had a childhood filled with Kodak moments and Hallmark Card sentiments didn't happen. That train had left the station many years ago, leaving me alone on the platform staring down the empty track of what could have been, but never was. While feeling sorry for myself for missing that train felt at once so comfortable and awful, I was able to let go of it because of what happened one day many years ago, long before this most awkward afternoon of my life.

Strangely enough, as I learned many years later, it took place on the same day as Jack Edward Byrd's forty-sixth birthday. A cold spring day in April when my pen ran out of ink.

Chapter 7

Running on Empty

Our lives begin to end the day
we become silent about the things that matter.
—Martin Luther King, Jr.

I was all of nineteen years old and a freshman in college on April 4, 1968 when it all started. I sat in the student union waiting for my girlfriend Janet to get out of class. We had met when we were thirteen years old in her father's garage to work on our freshman homecoming float with others in our class. I had no interest in making faux flowers out of tissue paper and stuffing them into chicken wire, but I was interested in getting out of the house to meet girls, so this was the price I had to pay. Four years later, we went off to college together.

Then we married. Each other.

We've been together ever since, producing two children who produced four children of their own. We don't like to brag, but we're a productive pair. I know others have produced more, but I like to think our quality control has been top-notch. We're even FDA certified. Never even had one recalled.

As I waited for Janet on that cold, cloudy spring afternoon, I took notes on one of the books from the reading list for a history course I was taking. Across the table from me sat our mutual friend, Carol, who had happened to be first runner-up to Miss Sheboygan, Wisconsin, the previous year. That was about as close to anyone famous as I was ever going to get. She was one of those attractive girls guys rarely ask out because they think beauty like hers has been long spoken for. It hadn't.

Carol, Janet, and I often hung out together in those early days of our relationship, that as of this writing, has seen forty-six Aprils come and go since our first one together. Janet spoke to Carol just last night on the phone. I could tell it was Carol by how Janet laughed. Loud, uproarious laughter, born of four-plus decades of marinating in a savored relationship together.

Back now to that first April in 1968. Carol was engrossed in her studying, as was I. Still an English major at this time, minoring in history, I soon reversed the two to minor in English instead. It was the only way I could avoid taking a course on Chaucer required of all English majors. Chaucer wrote in middle English, and the little I saw of it, scared me. Shakespeare was hard enough in Elizabethan English. What a wimp I was not to tackle middle English.

So instead of studying *The Canterbury Tales* that afternoon, I poured over the more readable *Rats, Lice and History–The Role of Disease in Changing the Course of Western Europe*. While taking notes, my pen ran out of ink. I didn't have a spare, so I interrupted Carol and asked her if she had an extra pen I could borrow.

"Sure," she said. "There should be one in my purse. Help yourself."

But I might lose a finger, I thought. Or maybe find something in there I had to ignore, or pretend I didn't know about without my face turning red. But I needed the pen and since Carol showed no interest in saving me from potential embarrassment, I pretended not to feel uncomfortable as I opened her purse. In those days, I spent a lot of time pretending I wasn't feeling what I was feeling.

As I opened her purse, hoping to make a quick strike to retrieve anything at all resembling a pen, I spotted a small mustard colored booklet, "*Have You Heard of the Four Spiritual Laws?*"

It grabbed my attention.

"Hey, Carol, what's this?" I asked with a great deal of curiosity. The title intrigued me. *Spiritual Laws?* How 1950s, I thought. Someone from the Eisenhower administration must have written this, or maybe a scriptwriter for *Leave it to Beaver* or *Father Knows Best*. It was the late 1960s after all, with free love, hippies, and Haight-Asbury. Laws were made to be broken, but now someone had written a booklet about four spiritual laws. It seemed out of place in the anti-war protest era of the time.

The Occupy Movement of the 2010s could take a lesson from the anti-war movement of the '60s and '70s. Frankly, the Occupy crowd needs to dress better for their protest to be taken seriously. They all look too much like those of us just occupying desks, factories, church pews, and suburban homes. My advice: grow longer hair, smoke something, stop shaving, stop showering, and then you'll start to look like a real protest movement.

Another thing that would help would be music. We had great anti-war, anti-everything music in the late '60s. But I can't think of one Occupy Movement song. Maybe Arlo Guthrie or Bob Dylan could help. I bet they'd love a chance to get out of the nursing home for a day to head down to a wheelchair-accessible recording studio.

Back again to 1968.

Carol stopped what she was doing, took out the mustard-colored booklet, and asked me the question on the cover, *Have You Heard of the Four Spiritual Laws?* I hadn't. The Ten Commandments, sure. Maybe these four spiritual laws were the abridged version. Maybe six of the commandments got demoted and re-classified as six suggestions, like Pluto going from a planet to a "dwarf planet" a few years ago.

She then went through each of the "laws" with me. The first one says, *"God loves you, and offers a wonderful plan for your life."* I always thought God loved humanity, but I never considered it was also an individual love, one directed at people personally. This was new to me. God, I thought, was too busy to be involved with an individual. After all, He's got to keep the solar system in order. I know he can multi-task, but this seemed a stretch to me. I had also never heard the idea that He has a "wonderful plan" for my life. I wondered what that plan was. It sounded a bit like an Amway presentation.

Law Two, Carol explained, states, "Man is sinful and separated from God. Therefore he cannot know and experience God's love and plan for his life." Yeah, that makes sense. I get that. If I were God, I wouldn't want to hang out with certain people I know, either. I never thought that being separated from God would interfere with His plan for my life. I never thought I could botch things up for God and interfere with this plan He has for me. And what exactly is this plan?

She went on to clarify the Third Law, which reads, "*Jesus Christ is God's only provision for man's sin. Through Him, you can know and experience God's love and plan for your life.*" But I thought if I were a good and moral person, that would please God. Isn't helping people enough, along with not robbing banks and things like that? I thought that if the good things outweighed the bad, I'd be okay. Carol showed me a simple diagram in which God was on the top, man was on the bottom, and there was a big gap in between. Jesus, she said, was the only way to bridge that gap. And there's that "plan" again. At age nineteen, I already had plans for my life, so I wondered what God's plan was.

The Fourth Law, Carol said, is, "*We must individually receive Jesus Christ as Savior and Lord; then we can know and experience God's Love and plan for our lives.*" This was the most startling "law" of all. I had no clue that this is how it worked. The first three laws were about what God does, but this one is about what I have to do. I had no idea that God wants a personal relationship with us.

Carol explained that God loves us, but we most often don't love Him back—which separates us from Him. He didn't give up on us, though. He sent His son Jesus to draw us back to Himself. He did this because He wants a personal relationship with us, but for this to happen, we have to want it, too.

Once she finished, I remember feeling incredulous and said something like, "Are you kidding me? Is this really true?" It was, she assured me. Carol then asked if I was interested in learning more, because if I was there was a meeting that night where a pastor friend of hers was speaking to explain all of this in more detail. Janet and I were welcome to come, she said.

And with that, I left to meet Janet after her class ended to walk back to our adjacent dorms.

"Janet," I said, "I've just heard the most incredible thing from Carol." I repeated back to her the best I could remember of the Four Spiritual Laws. I think I remembered only three of them, but I got the general idea. She was just as intrigued by this discovery as I was, so we decided to attend the meeting to which Carol invited us that Thursday evening.

I remember sitting in the meeting enthralled by a thin, older, white-haired man with glasses, Carol's pastor friend from Sheboygan, Wisconsin. Reverend Ellis Mooney. We later got to know him, and though Carol affectionately called him "Pops," Janet and I always referred to him as Reverend Mooney. Never "Ellis," like we do today with pastors, not even Pastor Ellis. No, it was Reverend Mooney. Even if he had asked us to call him Ellis, we could no more have felt comfortable doing this than we could have calling our social studies teacher from high school "Ron" if we ran into him near the canned vegetables in the grocery store. Actually, you'd be more likely to run into Ron in the beer and wine aisle.

Reverend Mooney talked that night about God's desire to have a personal relationship with us through his son, Jesus Christ, and how Jesus came to die for all our sins so we could have this kind of relationship with us. I remember thinking, *"Why haven't I heard this before?"* I mean, after all, I was already nineteen, had grown up in a mainline denominational church and its parochial grade school, and shouldn't I have known about everything by now? What an incredible thing I had been missing.

Carol's white-haired pastor friend from Sheboygan recounted miraculous stories from his life where Christ answered his prayers in remarkable ways that clearly showed he had a deeply personal relationship with Jesus. It was obvious Jesus had a deeply personal relationship with him.

"I want that, too," I thought.

When Reverend Mooney finished, he told us we too could have what he had, a personal relationship with Jesus, by confessing our sins and inviting Jesus into our lives as savior to take control of it. He asked us to close our eyes, and then told us if we wanted this same personal relationship, we should silently repeat after him a prayer he was going to say that would invite Jesus into our lives, and that would surrender our lives to him. When he finished, he told us to keep our eyes closed, but if we prayed this prayer, we should raise our hand. My hand went up like a space shuttle blast from Cape Canaveral. Out of the corner of one eye, I saw Janet's hand was raised as well.

Unlike others who have heard this same message for centuries, I had no concept of my own personal sin at the time. My concept of sin was as thin as a blade of grass—don't kill people, don't lie, and don't steal. It wasn't until I started to grow in my faith that I came to understand my sinful nature was more like a thousand-acre sod farm than a single blade of grass.

I wanted a relationship with Jesus out of greed and envy for what Ellis Mooney had. I wanted someone to care about me. I wanted someone to do what I asked them. I wanted someone to think about meeting my needs.

I want. I want. I want.

I wanted someone who didn't mind I was born out of wedlock. And above all, I wanted someone who had time for me. Who was never too busy or pre-occupied with cleaning the house, mowing the grass, or drinking the afternoon away with friends at the corner bar. Jesus seemed like He would be that for me (never considering until years later who I would be for Him). I decided to give this a try.

After leaving the meeting that evening in the student union, we noticed something very odd. All the TV's were turned on, which was unusual for this era long before CNN and the 24-hour news cycle of our present day. All the networks were broadcasting the late-breaking news of the assassination of Dr. Martin Luther King, Jr. earlier that afternoon. We all stood stunned, our eyes glued to the TV screens.

His life had ended in Memphis, Tennessee on April 4, 1968, the same day my life—my spiritual life—began in Eau Claire, Wisconsin. Janet and I met life the same day he met death. And as I learned many years later, April 4th was also the birth date of Jack E. Byrd, my birth father. He celebrated his forty-sixth birthday the same day I celebrated my spiritual birth, and which I'm now writing about forty-six years later.

The coincidence between these events still chills me.

One day, we will meet our physical death as Martin Luther King did, but because of the life Janet and I found that night, we live life differently now. We live knowing a God who chose to call an illegitimate and depressed nineteen-year-old to Himself must be a God who truly loves unconditionally. And that is the God I have spent time getting to know ever since.

The following fall, after that never-to-be-forgotten-April evening, Janet and Carol became roommates, and then a year after that, I replaced Carol as Janet's roommate when we got married. Carol married our friend Terry a year or two later, and the four of us have been friends ever since.

A number of years ago, Janet and I met Carol and Terry at a motel in north-central Wisconsin for a getaway weekend in the middle of January. While reminiscing about our college years, the events of that April evening in 1968 came up, at which point Carol reminded me of something I had forgotten.

"You left out one important part of what happened. Don't you remember the sport coat story? Remember what Pops said to everyone who committed their life to Christ that night? He told everyone who surrendered their life to Jesus to sometime in the next day or so to ask Jesus to reveal Himself in a personal way."

It all came back to me then. I had gone back to my dorm room that evening and prayed "God, if you are real, please show yourself to me. If what that old white-haired man said is really true, please show me."

Within a short time of my prayer, one of the guys on my floor knocked on my door.

"I need a sport coat for tomorrow night. Do you have one you could sell me?"

I did. A sport coat I had gotten when I was thirteen for my eighth-grade graduation that no longer fit my nineteen-year-old body. I had considered throwing it away in the garbage just a few days prior. He offered me twenty dollars for it, which at the time, felt more like $220. All for something I was ready to throw away. So I took his twenty dollars for the sport coat as an answer to my prayer that Jesus reveal Himself to me.

This, too, chills me when I think about it.

We need to remind each other of our own stories. Carol did that for me.

Her reminder evoked more reflection and caused me to think back to the risk she took when she went through the *Four Spiritual Laws* booklet with me so long ago. Carol, a relatively new believer in Jesus herself at the time, didn't have all the Christian jargon down yet, and as I later found out, was pretty nervous talking about Jesus. Yet she cared more for me and the state of my soul than she did about her own anxiety. She cared more for me than her worry about what I might think of her.

As the four of us sat around the motel pool this nostalgic night, thick condensation formed on the glass walls from the subzero cold of the outside meeting the warm air of the indoor pool.

"Just think, Carol, of the impact of what happened to us that night so long ago. Janet and I get married a few years later and now have two kids who become followers of Jesus themselves. And then our kids became instrumental in leading people to Christ in their sphere of influence.

"Jennifer toured with The Continentals the summer before her senior year of college, performing evangelistic concerts in the eastern US, Brazil, South Africa, and England. Then our son Michael, as part of a summer college missions trip, helped lead a distraught woman to Christ who was about ready to take her own life in Chicago."

"There will be people you will meet in heaven who have never heard of you, Carol, while on earth, but who will be able to trace their story, and their reason for being there to you. Back to the time you offered me a pen and told me about Jesus."

Another example came to mind just recently of the ripple effect we have on people. It's about Geraldine, my student aide when I was a teacher back in the '70s. She earned credit for helping me during her senior year in high school. We often talked about things going on in her life, and during one particularly bad stretch of difficulties for her, I told her about Jesus, much as Carol had told me. She responded to Jesus calling her to Himself and turned her life over to Him. It changed her, just as Jesus had changed me and everyone else who turns to Him.

Years later, she married and invited Janet and me to go out for dinner with her and her husband. We did this several times, then our lives drifted apart. We reconnected when I found out she was going to graduate from nursing school. Janet and I went to the ceremony. More time elapsed. Then we reconnected again at a funeral parlor, of all places. Her father and my father both had services in the same funeral home a day apart.

Each year, we exchanged Christmas cards, until one year several years ago, she wrote, "We're not sending Christmas cards out any-more—it's just gotten to be too much. So this card I'm sending you and Janet is the only one I'm sending this year."

She closed with a sentence that is forever engraved in my heart,

"Because of you, I have Jesus."

It's because of Jesus that Geraldine has Jesus.

I just played a small supporting role in the grand drama of Jesus calling people to Himself. It's a role I wish I would play more often. A role that Reverend Mooney and Carol played so well in my life.

After that last Christmas card, I again lost contact with Geraldine until Facebook came on the scene. From that, I learned she was having heart surgery. A surgery she was very worried about. I reminded her she has Jesus. She came through the operation fine, and several days before her release from the hospital, I drove eighty miles to visit her. We hadn't seen each other in years. We talked for about an hour, then I headed home.

I wondered at times why I had taken the journey, for it took up most of my day. I know I did it because I care for her, and I know Jesus cares for her. And perhaps I did it because Reverend Mooney once drove a lot farther for me, because he had Jesus and he wanted me and others to have Him, too. Maybe that's why. Maybe a little bit of Reverend Mooney rubbed off on me.

All of this makes me think of "What if..." questions. Not the "What if..." questions we ask ourselves when something bad happens, like "What if I had not been worrying about my son's illness, would I have plowed into that car at the stop sign?" I'm talking about the "What if..." questions we should ask when good things happen.

What if my pen had not run out of ink on that April afternoon in 1968?

What if I had decided to study somewhere else that day?

What if Janet and Carol had never become friends?

What if Reverend Mooney had said "That's too far for me to drive for a Thursday night meeting to talk to college kids who don't even go to my church, and whom I'll probably never see again."

What if Janet had not committed her life to Christ like I did?

What if my home life growing up had not been so bad that I wanted to go away to school as far away as reasonably possible, and I had ended up at a different college?

What if my guidance counselor in high school had not been able to pull some strings so I could get financial aid to go away to school?

What if none of these things had ever happened?

Where would I be now?

In 2002, I got a letter in the mail from my alma mater, what is now the University of Wisconsin–Eau Claire, telling me someone had nominated me for a Distinguished Alumnus Award for that year, and would I please fill out an application if I wanted to be considered. No thank you. I was too busy, and this kind of thing never meant much to me.

Janet encouraged me to fill it out, so after several months, I completed the application and sent it in. I wrote a lot about the mission work I did on trips to Mali in West Africa, and to Tajikistan in Central Asia. Surprisingly, I was one of three alums who were selected for this honor. The date was set and we were told to give a brief speech at a very nice reception following the university's graduation ceremony.

At the reception, Janet and I were assigned to the table hosted by the university chancellor. A nice enough man, and an interesting conversationalist with a decidedly liberal bent. Carol and her husband, Terry, were there, too. When it came time for my little five-minute speech, I talked about what the university meant to me, and how what I did in Mali and Tajikistan had its roots on this campus the day Martin Luther King, Jr. was killed. I mentioned the day he was assassinated was the same day I committed my life to Jesus at a meeting held in the very same building we were all in now.

I think the chancellor was expecting something else from my talk, but I felt such freedom to say what was on my heart in ways that were so natural and yet so unlike me. It was only through the grace of God that He reached down from Heaven to grab my heart because He wanted to spend time with me, because He wanted a relationship with me, and because He had a vision for me and saw what I could be many years down the road, that at age nineteen I could never imagine.

In using an empty pen and a very nervous First Runner-up Miss Sheboygan 1967, God reminds me that He uses unlikely means to further His kingdom, and I should be on the watch for where He is working, because He is in everything that is good, and right and true. And if God did all this to tell me about Himself and what I needed, I can depend on Him to continue to care for me, and to tell me the other things I need to become more the person He wants me to be, and more the person who reflects His image well.

Forty-six Aprils have come and gone since running on an empty pen and an empty life. The continuing challenge since that first April is what do I do with the rest of my life? How do I fill the emptiness? What kind of person should I be, given all the things that are wrong with me? Considering where I've come from, starting with my illegitimate birth, how can I use all this for some higher purpose?

Do I want to live like one of those coffee cups you see in small-town restaurants on streets with angle parking? Coffee shops that open at 6 a.m., where a sign on the front door boasts of their bottomless cup of coffee, where the more coffee you drink from your cup, the more the waitress fills it? Do I want a life where just as soon as one need is met, I find another to replace it? Where life is just a waitress filling my cup over and over again, and I keep making more and more trips to the bathroom?

There's got to be more to life than simply getting my needs met. Maybe I could live instead the way people did in another small town with angle parking on main street.

Bedford Falls, 1947.

Chapter 8

Calling Bedford 247

You haven't had a perfect day
until you've done something for
someone who can never pay you back.
—John Wooden

I love *It's a Wonderful Life*, the 1947 Frank Capra Christmas movie
starring Jimmy Stewart and Donna Reed. While you can see it on
TV almost weekly each December, it's best viewed in a movie
theater, uninterrupted by commercials for pain relievers and Toyota.
Several years ago, we took our son, his wife, and their three kids to the
Times Theater for their first theater viewing of the film. Located in an
older residential area of our city, the Times is a relic from an era when
people walked to their neighborhood movie house. Our grandkids
enjoyed the film, but their parents couldn't get past the tattered
corduroy-covered theater seats, gum on the peeling paint of the concrete
floor, and the odd odor coming from a nearby seat.

Picky. Picky. Picky.

It's all part of the ambiance you can't find at a nineteen-screen, 3-D
multiplex. We've been back several times to the Times to see *It's a
Wonderful Life* with the grandkids, leaving their killjoy parents at
home. They love it—or could it be they loved the popcorn and candy
we bought?

One of my favorite scenes in the movie is when Jimmy Stewart,
playing George Bailey, comes home on Christmas Eve after learning
his Uncle Billy has misplaced $8,000 from the savings and loan George
manages in Bedford Falls. George got very upset in the previous scene

and roughed up Uncle Billy, shaking him by the collar, shouting, "Where's the money, you silly old fool? Don't you know what this means? It means scandal, and one of us is going to prison, and it's not going to be me!"

When George comes home he finds his wife, Mary (Donna Reed) decorating their Christmas tree, one of the children practicing a Christmas Carol on the piano, and another of the kids sick in bed. Except for George, it's a Kodak moment before Kodak had moments. It's Christmas after all, with tinsel on the tree and Christmas carols coming from the piano. George, however, is visibly upset, and has sharp exchanges with his kids. His anger eventually overcomes him.

"What's the matter, George?" Mary asks.

"Nothing's the matter," he bristles.

This reminds me of what I mentioned in the first chapter, "People are Like Houses." The opening George was giving Mary to his "house" was not readily apparent. His words certainly didn't match his behavior. At first, Mary doesn't pick up on the incongruity, but she does later when she switches from trusting his words to seeing reality in his actions and his out-of-character snarly mood. There is something wrong, terribly wrong, for George to be acting this way.

George's anger forces Mary into the position of protecting the kids from their own father.

"George, why must you torture the children? Why don't you..."

She bites her tongue and doesn't finish the sentence. No need to, for we can finish it for her. *Why don't you just get out of here and don't come back until you can be civil to me and the children? Why don't you stop ruining our Christmas?* Wisely, Mary stops herself and says nothing. Sometimes the best words are the words we keep to ourselves.

With a sweeping motion of his arm, George then turns and knocks to the floor a model bridge resting on a table, symbolic of his dashed dream of leaving Bedford Falls for adventure beyond his sleepy little hometown. Like an alcoholic vowing to never drink another drop, George apologizes to Mary and the children, but his anger soon erupts again and he leaves the house.

The camera then closes in on Mary as she picks up the telephone with the children gathered around her.

"Bedford 247, please."

Mary doesn't know what's wrong with her husband, but she knows someone who might—George's business partner, Uncle Billy. She picks up the phone to call him to see if he knows what she doesn't. To care well for others sometimes means we have to go around obstacles, to pursue people, to even become a bit of a detective in trying to figure out what's going on, which is exactly what Mary does.

When Mary asked, "George, what's the matter?" he replied with "Nothing's the matter…" and then went off on a rant. His rant tells us there *IS* something the matter. Actions tell the truth; words many times do not. Mary realizes she's getting nowhere with George, so she makes a mid-course correction to investigate more by calling her husband's co-worker, Uncle Billy.

"Is Daddy in trouble?" the oldest boy asks while Mary waits for Bedford 247 to answer.

"Yes, Pete."

"Shall I pray for him?" one of the girls asks.

"Yes, Janie. Pray very hard."

"Me, too?"

"Yes, you too, Tommy," Mary responds as someone answers her phone call.

"Hello? Uncle Billy?"

This is the last we see of Mary and Uncle Billy until the end of the film.

For while George is off dealing with his fears and identity crisis, Mary and Uncle Billy are working behind the scenes to care for George.

That's how it is sometimes with caring for others; it's done behind the scenes, out of the spotlight. Moreover, care sometimes comes from unlikely sources, as it does in the movie, from Uncle Billy himself. He's the one responsible for the missing money, but George is taking the hit for him.

At the end of the movie, we learn that Uncle Billy must have told Mary about the lost cash and the bank examiner's visit. We see in the last scene that once Mary knows what the problem is, she acts and enlists the help of what seems like all of Bedford Falls to care for her husband. They step forward with the money needed to make up for the $8,000 Uncle Billy lost.

While all that is going on, George comes to realize the important role he's played in the lives of so many of those in his community. It doesn't matter anymore to George if he does go to prison, for he comes to appreciate that family and friends are the most important things in life.

I'd like to live in Bedford Falls, not just because it's a small town with angle parking on the main street, but because of how people who live there care for each other. I think God had Bedford Falls in mind when he created the church. A church should be like Bedford Falls, where we look out for each other. Where people care for those like Uncle Billy, who copes with the death of his wife by drinking way too much, way too often. A church should be a place where people think of the less fortunate, as George Bailey does in giving out home loans to people who are turned down by old man Potter and his bank because of their credit score, before they even had credit scores.

Bedford Falls shows us what it's like for a community to care for people who even seem to have it all together, like George Bailey. Mary Bailey knew something was wrong with her husband when he came home from work on Christmas Eve. She doesn't know what to do at first, but that doesn't stop her. She picks up the phone and calls Bedford 247.

Good things usually happen when we make phone calls. Bad things often occur when we receive them. Calling Bedford 247 is a pivotal point in *It's a Wonderful Life*, for it begins the chain of events alerting people from the community that George needs $8,000 to stay out of jail. When the need is presented, the community responds with what George needs. Sometimes church is like that, and when it is, it makes God smile.

* * * * *

A similar story is playing itself out right now at our church, a real life story about our friend, Jill—a single woman, never married, who at age fifty almost overnight becomes a mom to four children, ages eight and under. For over three years, Jill had been developing a relationship with her next door neighbors, a couple and their four kids, plus two grandparents, all under the roof of a very small house. As Jill befriended the adults in the household, it became increasingly apparent that their various addictions interfered with their ability to care for the children.

The relationship Jill developed with the parents and grandparents over time allowed Jill to have numerous heart-to-heart talks with them about the poor choices they were making in life. Because she invested time building relationships with the adults, she earned the right to have difficult conversations with them about how their choices were affecting the children. She explained how a life of faith in God could get them out of the mess they had created for themselves. They engaged in spiritual conversations with Jill, and received her words well, but never acted on them. Meanwhile, the poor choices made by the adults in the house continued to adversely affect the children in the house.

During this three-year period of building a relationship with her neighbors, the children gradually began spending significant amounts of time with Jill. When she came home from work, the children would run to her car and fight over who would open the door for Jill. They helped her carry in groceries from the car. Jill would ask them about their day, they'd answer, then give her hugs. When they saw Jill in the yard, they came over to be with her, sometimes to play on the front porch with Jill the board games she bought for them. They couldn't get enough of her. Hugs both ways abounded.

As Jill saw more of the dysfunction in their home life, she could understand why the kids wanted to be with her. The parents and grandparents began to tell Jill the children needed help, help they themselves felt unable to provide. The grandparents were the primary tenant in the flat next door, and eventually over frustration with their adult children's addictions, evicted them and their four children.

When Jill asked where they were going to move, the father said he planned to get a tent and live in a state park with the kids and their mother. When it became obvious decisions like this were harming the children, Jill stepped in and called Child Protective Services. They came one afternoon and investigated what Jill reported, during which time the parents readily admitted they did not have the wherewithal to properly care for their children.

The father recommended that Jill take custody of the kids. Jill agreed. Child Protective Services also agreed, and with no objection from anyone, by 11 p.m. that night, the four children moved and were sound asleep in Jill's two-bedroom, 600-square-foot upper flat. Instant family.

This arrangement was viewed as temporary custody by everyone. When Jill bought her home, she had done so with the intention of using it in some way to make a positive difference in her neighborhood, but she never pictured it would take the form of taking in four foster kids. She never imagined they would capture her heart as they had. The three boys moved into Jill's spare bedroom, the girl took over Jill's bedroom, and Jill bonded with her living room couch, where she slept each night.

Jill did not want to do any of this apart from the county's childcare system. This required getting certified as a foster-care parent, which meant taking classes on Saturday for several weeks. Until Jill passed the certification requirements, no financial assistance to care for the children would be forthcoming. Instead of having just one mouth to feed, she now had five, and with school starting in September, Jill's credit card balance began to rise. When her Sunday school community group learned of this in late November, they took up a collection for Jill and her kids. Many people contributing a little, raised over $1,300 in just a few weeks to pay off credit card bills for expenses incurred, and for Christmas gifts for the children who knew little of Christmas.

As Jill began telling people what was happening, friends, and friends of friends, began to get involved. "So many people wanted to know how they could help," Jill said. "Some gave us Target gift cards, another person donated a crib, high chair, and plastic dishes. A friend gave us a set of bunk beds, and another friend drove an hour away to pick it up, bring it my house, and put it together for the kids. One family gave us their minivan—just gave it to us. In two months' time, we went from not having much of what we needed to having all our needs taken care of."

Others began showing up to babysit the children so Jill could continue working in her Grace Place ministry to men, women, and their families affected by same-sex attraction. Others came to watch the kids while Jill took classes to get her foster parenting license. Even teenage children of friends came to help Jill by watching and playing with the children so she could get other things done around the house. The teenage helpers would hang out with the four kids outside, so they could draw with sidewalk chalk, play catch, run through the sprinkler, and paint fingernails. Five or six of them would watch the foursome so Jill could do laundry, cook meals, and mow the lawn.

Jill also spoke of the role her parents played. "My mom and dad have been an incredible blessing; they have been invaluable. They have stepped up to the plate as awesome grandparents and taken the role very seriously. Who would have thought that two years ago when I moved them from California to Milwaukee to care for them, that they would be caring for me and the kids in such incredible ways? They are loving this. Each Tuesday, they come over for dinner and Mom cooks the meal. They often take the kids on mornings or afternoons so I can do other things."

"At one point, I had twenty people on my list who volunteered to watch the kids when I wasn't available, and each of them was required to pass a background check, which they all readily agreed to do. They fell in love with the kids as they stepped up to help, and I began to feel less and less alone in this," Jill said.

"One evening, I posted on Facebook how I was spending the night picking lice out of the kids' hair they had picked up from their class-mates at school. One of my friends saw my post at 1:00 a.m. and came over and helped me de-louse everyone," Jill recounted. "Others cooked meals for us, which is probably the most ongoing need we have. It's one thing to cook just for yourself, but to cook for yourself and four children is another. I wish God would have given me the gift of loving to cook, but he didn't.

"Another thing that happened involved a fence I wanted to put up. I purchased all the materials and was going to put it up myself, but caring for the kids kept me from this project. When people from our church heard about it, nine men came over to put up the fence for me and the kids."

Word spread to other parts of the country about the needs of this instant family. At Christmas time, Jill's aunt and uncle and their two adult sons living in Texas decided to forgo buying Christmas gifts for each others' families, and to instead use the money to buy presents for

Jill's kids. "This was a Christmas they will never forget," Jill said. It was a beautiful Christmas morning watching them open their presents. They had never been loved on like this before. It was really sweet to see them lavished upon like this."

One of the kids had a birthday the summer they moved in with Jill, so she threw a party for Amy, the 8-year-old girl who had never had a birthday party before. Thirty adults and children showed up to celebrate. They hugged her and told her how glad they were to get to know her. With tears in her eyes, Amy told Jill how special she felt for the first time in her life. Her brother Nathan later told Jill that night through tears that his dad had completely forgotten his birthday last year, and they didn't celebrate it at all. So when his birthday came, Jill threw a birthday party for Nathan, too, and another thirty people came to honor him. That happened the day after he broke his collarbone at a church activity.

"Even that night at church, here we were in a crisis. I had four children at the event and one of them breaks his collarbone. What do you do? Our youth pastor carried Nathan to the van. Another man took charge of the other three children and sent me off to the hospital with the one. Someone drove us so I could sit in the back seat with Nathan. Our children's pastor and her husband took the other kids to their home to watch them.

"I didn't have to ask for help. People saw the need and just stepped in. Ben, our worship director, is an EMT, which I didn't know. He took off his t-shirt and made a temporary sling for Nathan to wear to the hospital. It was crazy cool to see how people just stepped up to help."

The emotional effect on the children in leaving their parents and moving in with Jill was significant. Jill noted, "The kids came with a huge lack of nurture. Every child comes with a need to be heard, to be known, to be able to ask questions. At one point, the oldest of the four, Amy, told her counselor, 'Jill's lap isn't big enough for all of us. The

two younger ones get lap time, but my brother Nathan and I don't.'"
The counselor in turn told Jill that because of all the children had been
through, the most important thing the kids needed was more of her.
They needed hugs, nurture, and to be heard. All of these had formed a
big vacuum in their lives up to this point.

For Jill to give more of herself to the kids, some things had to slide,
like house cleaning. One Sunday morning, Jill shared this with her adult
Sunday school community, at which point several women volunteered
to come over to Jill's upper flat and take care of basic house cleaning
tasks. Several have come back multiple times. Others have painted. As
increasingly more people in Jill's circle of friends learned of what she
was taking on, more people began stepping up to the plate to give Jill
what she needed, which in turn gave her more time for the kids.

Toward the end of the year, Child Protective Services told Jill that
if she wanted to continue custody of the children, she would have to
find other housing arrangements. "We had four months of bonding in a
600-square-foot, two-bedroom apartment," Jill said, "but that was going
to have to change."

It was okay for the three boys to be in one room, and Amy to be in
one room, but Jill needed a bedroom for herself, according to her case
worker. They told her she would have to move no later than the end of
February, or lose custody of the kids. Jill thought maybe she could
convert her duplex into a one-family home, but she needed the income
from the lower flat to help pay her mortgage. So that option would not
work. Selling her duplex and buying a house also wasn't an option
because the balance on her mortgage was more than the value of the
house.

Jill began looking for three-bedroom apartments, spending hours
and hours online looking through housing websites. She drove past
homes and apartments, but could find nothing in a safe neighborhood
for less than $1,300 to $1,400 month, well above what she could afford.

Besides, it was going to be difficult to find someone to rent to a single mom with four young kids and a dog.

The clock was ticking and there were no prospects in sight. "I didn't know how God was going to answer my prayer for a place for all of us to live," Jill wondered.

One day, a man in Jill's Grace Place ministry offered to sell his house to Jill at a below-market price. This seemed to have possibilities, but even at below market value, it was still more than Jill could afford. It was then that another man in Jill's church and Sunday School community group, James, approached Jill and said, "You've shared with us about the sacrifice you are making for those kids and the way you are caring for them. Since you have stepped up to the plate for them, it's time for some of us to step up to the plate with you."

"I cried when he said that," Jill said.

He went on to describe a plan he had to form an LLC of at least ten investors who would buy the property offered to Jill, and then lease it back to her. There would be different classes of investors, each with varying amounts of skin in the game. All investment dollars would be used for a down payment, together with a mortgage from a lending institution to buy the house.

James put a lot of work into coming up with this plan, including contacting a banker who knew Jill's story, and was receptive to putting together a loan for the LLC. One important issue with the house offered to Jill was that it was a duplex, which would have to be converted to a single-family home and be costly to retrofit. Time was running out and Jill was beginning to feel the pressure of the impending deadline to move.

Jill continued with her story. "I wasn't sure at this point that God was remembering our need. But then one day, another friend, Tom, was sitting in church thinking about the complications of the LLC James was putting together, and all the work he had already put into it, knowing there would be more issues to iron out. It was at that point in church he felt a whisper from God, 'This would be a lot less complicated if YOU were to buy the house yourself and lease it back to Jill.' Tom said his first response to God was a resounding 'No.' God was gentle with him, though, and whispered back, 'C'mon now. Work with me on this. You can do this. You can buy the house. You've got savings you can use that aren't earning much interest anyway. Buy the house outright, lease it back to Jill at a rate she can afford, and you'll still get a small rate of return. Look at the good it will accomplish for Jill and the kids. Trust me on this one, okay?'

"With that, Tom leaned over to his wife in church and whispered in her ear what God had whispered in his, 'I sense God telling me we should buy that house for Jill and lease it back to her.' On the way home from church, Tom and his wife talked about it, and within a few days, agreed to this plan and called me about it. I was stunned at their offer and cried, as I often do when I see God's provision in my life..

"Given the complications with converting the duplex offered to me into a one family, Tom asked me if I would be open to considering other homes. I was, so Tom and I both began looking online for other properties in the same price range. Tom called a realtor friend, Dan, who gave him advice as to which parts of town were declining in value, and which areas were on the upswing. Following Dan's advice, Tom searched and found nothing in the price range of the original duplex offered to me. So he gulped and expanded the search by raising the upper limit of the asking price. Soon after that, about eight properties came up in the search that would work. Dan advised against four of them, and agreed to schedule showings on the other four.

"I was going to be out of town when Tom and his wife could view the four properties. Before I left, I drove past each house; one of them in particular stood out. I remember thinking, 'Oh, I really like this one. I hope Tom and his wife do, too. I would really like that house and the neighborhood.'

"Dan took Tom and his wife through the four properties, and the last one they looked at that morning was the one I really wanted, and it was the one Tom and his wife like the most, too. They said there was no comparison between it and the other three. It required the least amount of work to move into. That very morning, they wrote an offer, which was soon accepted. Tom told me, 'I trust Dan's judgment on real estate maters, but I'm surprised that I spent more time picking out my cell phone than I did buying this house. I truly feel this is from God.'

"We then had the inspection of the house prior to closing. When the inspector learned how Tom was buying this house for the kids and me to rent, he reduced his fee. When Dan first learned of why we needed a house, he waived his fee. When the plumber came to do some work to correct a few things from the inspection report, he gave a discount. All these people were caring for me and the kids with their finances. I know the rent I'm paying Tom and his wife is about half of what they could get if they rented it to someone on the open market. I am so blessed.

"When people learned we finally had a place to move to, I put a post on Facebook that on a particular Saturday I could use some help getting our new place ready to move in. Fifteen people showed up that day! People from my current church, my old church, and some people I haven't seen in years. They removed wallpaper, painted the entire interior of the house, tore up an old rug. They did all kinds of things to get the place ready. This was so encouraging.

"As moving day approached, several people who said they were going to help had to drop out at the last minute. So I posted another request for help on Facebook and forty people showed up to help. Four of them were people I didn't even know—they just happened to be friends of friends who wanted to help. This was so encouraging. One of the new neighbors across the street brought over a huge pot of chili to feed all the people helping us move in."

All these different people were caring for Jill and her tribe of four in many different ways. So many people felt a nudging from God to do what they could to care. One example sticks out in particular of how a friend, Debra, cared for Jill by doing nothing.

While at church one day with thoughts of the kids on her mind, Jill accidentally backed the minivan given to her into a car in the church parking lot. She didn't know who the car belonged to, so she left a note apologizing for what happened and asked the owner to call her so she could contact her insurance company. One more thing to deal with, one more hassle, one more item to add to Jill's already lengthy to-do list. Shortly after this mishap, Debra approached Jill in church and identified herself as the person Jill had backed into. Debra told Jill not to worry about it, that she had some other bodywork she needed done, and if what Jill had damaged wasn't too expensive to repair, Debra would take care of it.

"But I have insurance, Debra," Jill said. "I can take care of it." She repeated this several times. Later, when estimates came in for the damage Jill caused, Debra again told Jill not to be concerned and that she would take care of everything. No need to get insurance involved. I suspect Debra sensed how overloaded Jill was with the kids, and how the stress of dealing with an insurance company would only add to the tension. She cared for Jill by not doing what she was entitled to—having Jill make her car whole again.

"I felt so released when Debra told me she'd take care of every-thing," Jill shared.

When you drill down on all the care Jill and the children received, it really is God at the heart of the care. He used ordinary people in extraordinary ways. Take her new home for example. Jill says, "This house has been a blessing is so many ways. We have four bedrooms now. I had been looking for a three bedroom. The kids now each have their own space they didn't have before. We have a fireplace, which they never had before, and which has always been a dream of mine.

Every Friday night, we have family movie night, where we eat pizza, and watch a movie by firelight in front of the fireplace.

"Another blessing is the new school district the kids are in. The other day Amy came home from school and said, 'It's my favorite place to be.' My ego took a little jolt with that one, but I was so glad she felt this way. The other school she was in before we moved had so many problems. It was in the lowest ranking district in the state of Wisconsin.

"Her new school is among the highest, and it's becoming another source of badly needed stability. The teachers have been phenomenal. The kids made friends the very first day, and they changed from dreading school to loving it. I love it that my kids now love school. Our neighbors have been a blessing, too. When word got out where we were moving, I got a call from my friend, Teri, who said, 'Your new house is only three houses away from where we live! Would you like me to email the fifty people on our neighborhood association mail list to see who can help you move in?'"

How can all this care for Jill and her four children be anything but God conducting a grand symphony of care-giving, using "musicians," many of whom do not know each other, each playing their individual part in producing a beautiful piece of music that brings glory to God as both composer and conductor? No one person being anymore important than the other—the violins, the oboes, French horn, cello, kettle drum, trumpets and trombones, flutes and bassoon—all making beautiful music together.

Watching the performance are those captivated by the wonder of it all. Jill describes the social worker assigned to her case as being deeply moved by the care the church and friends have provided her and the children. She told Jill her situation is the only one that encourages her to keep going in her career, for it's so uplifting to see the care that has come out of the woodwork for the four children, when so many other cases and stories are just the opposite and filled with heartache. She plans to write an article about Jill's situation for their foster parent newsletter because she wants other church communities to see how people can make a positive difference in the lives of kids.

The caseworker told Jill, "I love coming to your house because I get filled up to keep doing what I am doing by what is happening in your story, and all the people who are involved in caring for you and the kids."

When I asked Jill what taking in the four children has meant to her, she gave a long and thoughtful pause and said, "I'm a fifty-year-old single woman who got really used to living an independent, self-sufficient life. I have a hard time asking anyone for help, not because I didn't want it, but because I felt I had to be self-sufficient. I have this driving need to be competent, because I think I found my value in that. This whole experience with the kids has brought about an incredible learning experience for me.

"First, it's taught me it's okay to be a person in need. I've learned how there can be a real depth in relationship and connection with people in having them step in to meet the needs you have, and the connection it creates, not just with me, but with the kids, too. Before the kids, I realized I was living much of my life alone. I realized God wants me to live in community, and part of living in community is admitting I can't do all of this myself. There's a depth of intimacy that occurs when we let someone help meet a need we have.

"I've never regretted taking in the children, but there are days when I'm exhausted and just don't know what to do. So I have a list of friends I'll text to ask them to pray for God's strength for me because I am just spread so thin. People have been very faithful to do this. Having the four kids has changed my life. It has made my life rich. I'm learning about my propensity to be selfish, and to instead set aside my own needs for a time. I've learned to dig deeper to try and understand what may be behind a tantrum one of the kids may be having. They make me laugh. They make me cry. This has all been hugely life-giving for me. I love that my house is filled with their noise. When I was in my thirties, I gave up on the notion that I would ever have children. I understand how these kids need me, but I have also needed them. They have breathed things into my life that I wasn't even aware at the time I needed."

And so it is with caring for others. It breathes life into our lungs and meets a need we didn't know we had until we take a risk and extend ourselves to others. It broadens our lives far more than an around-the-world cruise, for it exposes us to the stories of others and invites us to bless them with what God has blessed us. When we bless others collectively, it brings out the best in us, for it motivates us to care in community in ways we might otherwise not do individually.

Caring for others can be exhausting and at once life-giving, as it is for my friend Jill. Most of us aren't given the assignment of raising four foster kids, but God gives us all an assignment to care for others in one form or another. Like being gracious to the difficult relative at Thanksgiving because we share the same ancestors, or listening to the person in our circle of friends who never stops talking, and whom we want to run from. But we stay, and nod, and pretend we're interested because we imagine their loneliness and the void that must be in their heart and how sad it must be.

These and countless other ways to care for people bring out the best in us as we look beyond our own needs. And when the best of us comes out, it makes God smile.

Chapter 9

Moving from *What If* to *Even If*

I wonder if my friend Jill worries since she became an instant parent of four kids through the foster care system. Parenthood, after all, brings many opportunities to feed the fear virus that runs through one's veins. Fear of kids getting hurt, killed, or bullied. Will they make it in life? Will they ever learn to behave, to clean their rooms, or treat their siblings with respect? What if a son never gets the hang of multiplying fractions? What if he never gets a hit in Little League? What if a daughter never gets invited to a sleepover?

For some, fear and anxiety is a debilitating medical condition requiring medication. For most, fear is something that gnaws away at us from time to time, often in the background. Psychologists tell us fear is the most basic of all emotions, that when you get right down to it, we're all afraid of something. People who are controlling are full of fear. People-pleasers are motivated by fear. Angry people and those with an exaggerated sense of their own importance are often driven by fear.

Sometimes worry can be a good thing. It was for me when I left the security of teaching teens, which I loved, for a commissioned sales job in an industry I knew nothing about. It was fear that partially propelled me out of education. Fear that I wasn't providing for my family, and that our credit card debt would mount as our children grew older. I worried I would become cynical like some of my colleagues in the faculty lounge who whined about the kids and the administration, both of whom I enjoyed. While these worries were part of my decision to leave a career in education, I left mainly because I felt a stirring within me that I could accomplish more.

I had been teaching for over seven years, and had gotten to the point where I thought I was going to be about as good a teacher as I ever was going to be. I was ready for something else. That something else turned out to be a twenty-five-year career as an executive recruiter, or "headhunter," which I thoroughly loved. I was blessed to have gotten off to a good start in this profession because of fear. Let me explain.

One of the attractions of the job for me was the notion that the more placements I made, the more money I would earn. My salary was not dependent on a teachers' union contract that dictated what I would make. There was a risk, however. What if I worked really, really hard, and still didn't make any placements? What if market forces prevented me from succeeding? What if I wasn't smart enough to learn the business? There were quite a few "What if's" in those days. The fear of not making any money was a strong motivator for me, because I had no plan B if this new career didn't work out. The fear motivated me to work hard because I was afraid we'd go broke if I didn't.

While I got off to a good start in my new profession, I remember thinking it was all going to come to an abrupt end. My house of cards was going to come tumbling down once people figured out I didn't really know what I was doing. It took about two years before my motivation gradually transitioned from fear to confidence that I could do the job. Fear can be a good motivator over the short haul, but it's a terrible way to live long-term. When we worry, we live in the future, thinking about calamity that could befall us. Because we're not living in the present, we miss out on the richness of the here and now.

I remember worrying about not preserving the present for the future when our son played high school basketball. A number of parents in those days religiously videotaped their sons' exploits on the court, long before smartphones were available, and when a camcorder weighed as much as a 40-pound sack of potatoes and handled just as awkwardly. Worried I wasn't the father I wanted to be, I borrowed a camcorder and tripod from a friend to record my son's last basketball game as a senior in high school. It was a terrible experience.

I spent so much time fiddling with the camera, adjusting the settings, zooming in and out, and looking through the viewfinder, that I missed out on the moments unfolding right before my eyes. Trying to preserve what I was watching now for some future viewing drove me to distraction from enjoying the wonder of the present. I was drained at the end of the evening, not because of the game, but because of all the energy I expended trying to record the moment to enjoy later in the future. What a waste.

The present is its own reward, its best reward. Sure, plan for the future, do what you can now. Be wise about tomorrow. But then let it go. If we let the future be the future, and the present be the present, we'll enjoy both so much more. One caveat though—don't confuse lack of worry with lack of planning.

Lack of planning is just plain dumb. We will worry less if we plan more. Worry is an emotion, and like any emotion, it is a reaction to something. Planning, however, is cognitive. Planning anticipates, it initiates. Worry reacts. I have life insurance so if I die before my wife, she'll be provided for. I don't worry about death, but I know it's going to happen. I know my car will last longer if I periodically change its oil. That's planning and it helps me worry less.

We can't plan away all problems to end worry and the "what ifs" of life. When we dwell on the "what ifs," it is sometimes about control. If we choose to worry—and many times, worry is a choice—it creates the illusion that we can change undesired outcomes. If we just plan well enough for the "what ifs," we may be able to avoid difficulties. Yet we all know deep inside that we don't have nearly as much control as we think we do.

When my son Michael was in college and got his semester's work done way ahead of time, it was to control a big "what if" in his life. "What if I get sick" started a chain reaction of thought patterns, beginning with fearing inability to complete course requirements, which led to fear of poor grades, leading to his ultimate fear, losing his scholarship. But, even if he lost his scholarship, so what? He would figure out a way to pay for college. He could work a semester, borrow money from his parents—I should say, his mother. He could transfer to a cheaper school. His graduation might be delayed for a year or two, but so what? Even if the worst happened, he'd still be okay. And while the "what if" scenario he played out in his mind was certainly possible, how probable was it? Not very. All that is possible is not all that is probable.

This "what if/even if" experience he went through as a college junior served him well ten years later when he was on the verge of becoming a father. As Michael and his wife Hope neared the end of her pregnancy, a complication developed. Notice I said her pregnancy. I don't understand couples who announce *we're* pregnant. It is only the singular female who is pregnant. Honestly. Look it up. Maybe it's me, but I think we have a serious pronoun problem here.

The pregnancy problem came to everyone's attention during Hope's second ultrasound of the twin boys growing inside her. Grant was not growing at the same rate as his brother George. This was so serious a condition that the doctor put Hope on complete bed rest for two weeks at home, hoping Grant would catch up. But another exam after two weeks showed Grant still lagging further behind his brother. At that point, the doctor explained the severity of the problem to my son and daughter-in-law. She explained Grant wasn't getting the nutrients he needed from the placenta he shared with his brother, and if this continued, the result would be fatal for Grant.

The doctor presented them with two options. One was to do nothing, in which case one of the boys would most likely live and go on to be a full-term baby, while the other would surely die. The second option was to admit Hope to the hospital for complete bed rest and closely monitor the boys' growth in the womb, preparing for any emergency action that might need to be taken. They immediately rejected the first option, so off to the hospital they went for Hope to rest, and hopefully for Grant to grow.

Two weeks into Hope's hospital stay, now at week thirty-one of gestation, the situation took a turn for the worse. I was at work and Michael came into my office to give me an update. As he slumped down in a chair in front of my desk, staring at the floor, he was the most distraught as I've ever seen him. He lifted his ashen face to tell me what the doctors were telling him, that the blood flow from the placenta through the umbilical cord to George was normal, but the rate of blood flow to Grant continued to lag, and at one point, nearly stopped altogether.

The doctors were very concerned that the blood flow between the placenta and Grant could even reverse, which would lead to his immediate death. The doctors determined they had to act soon because the risk of losing Grant was getting too high. They said that to give the babies the best chance of survival, they needed to get out of the womb within the next twenty-four hours, either through induced labor or a C-section.

The prospects for a happy outcome were not great. Babies born at thirty-one weeks have a much higher mortality rate than those born after the normal thirty-nine weeks. This was one of the scariest moments of my life, and I can't imagine how worried Michael and Hope must have been.

As a father, everything inside of me wanted to say, "Don't worry, things are going to turn out okay. Lots of people are praying about this. It'll be fine." Everything within me wanted to say this because it came out of my own fear that things might not turn out well. It would have looked like support and compassion on the outside, but it would have come from a place of pre-occupation with my own feelings of dread. Besides that, it would not have been true. I would have lied to my son. Things we worry about don't turn out well just because we will them to. This isn't reality. God doesn't owe it to us to keep our babies alive.

So I sat in silence for a time. Sometimes silence is the best response. Instead of my "things will be okay" comment, after a very long pause I said instead, "Michael, regardless of what happens, whatever it might be, you and Hope will be okay."

We talked about what if the worst did occur. It would be terribly painful, but he and Hope would make it. They would survive. And God's grace would be there for them, and for all of us, when we needed it. Leaning forward with elbows on his knees spread apart, and with hands clasped together while he stared at the floor, Michael slowly and silently nodded his head in acknowledgment of this difficult truth. And he really did know, I'm convinced of it. He had left the "What if" life behind to become an "Even if" young man. I was so proud of him.

The next morning, Friday, February 8, the doctor induced labor, hoping she wouldn't need to do a C-section. Hope was as strong as she is beautiful through this. All during her hospital stay, two monitors rested on her abdomen to monitor the heartbeats of each boy. Throughout the day and night, a nurse would come in and monitor the monitor. Sometimes at a very inconvenient time, like during *Oprah*.

Eventually, contractions started to come. As they came more quickly late in the afternoon, nurses wheeled Hope in her bed out of her room, past us on the way to the delivery room. Following close behind was our son and Hope's sister, both dressed in scrubs and ready for whatever would happen next.

As she was wheeled past us, our daughter-in-law looked as worried as her husband had the day before in my office. And why not, she had never been through this before. Her distress became our distress. We sometimes forget Hope is not our daughter, that she has parents (and they are great people), but it just always feels like Hope is our own flesh and blood. We love her no less than our own children. I sometimes mistakenly introduce her to people as our daughter. To see our Hope worried made Janet and me even more concerned.

This drama was all about seeing our children go through difficulty and anxiety, where life and death hang in the balance, and there is absolutely nothing you can do about it except pray. The reality of what they faced became our reality. Their worry, our worry. What if both babies died? What if George lived and Grant died? The sorrow of the latter would far outweigh the joy of the former.

Do Michael and Hope have the spiritual resources to deal with this possibility? Do we? I had to remind myself of what Michael and I talked about. "Even if" the worst happened, we would all still be okay. God's grace and comfort would be there when we needed it most.

For what seemed like an endless wait, which we later learned was only an hour, Hope's sister came flying into the waiting room, still dressed in her scrubs, sobbing with joy as she announced the boys both made it, they both looked great, both were healthy, and both were doing what newborns are supposed to do twenty minutes into their lives outside the womb. George, the first born whom I would come to call "Buster," weighed in at 3 pounds 15 ounces, followed two minutes later by Grant, who slid out and tipped the scales at 1 pound 15 ounces. I would later call him "Moose." Our son counted sixteen people in the delivery room, all crying and hugging each other, because the "What if" everyone dreaded did not happen.

Soon after the boys were born, our daughter Jennifer arrived with her husband Tim; we now had the whole family there. We heard Hope was hungry so Tim left to get pizza. When he returned, Hope was wheeled in, and we all squeezed into her little room. Before digging into the pizza and the birthday cupcakes Jennifer made, we sang *Happy Birthday.*

Our off-key rendition, I think, caused a heart monitor in the next room to malfunction, but the song never had so much meaning as it did at that moment. It was indeed a happy birthday. We all paused to pray and savor the moment. Two little lives, two God-breathed souls, had just been given to our family. All of us gathered around Hope's bed, taking it all in, letting the memory of the moment engrave itself onto our hearts.

Speechless. Awestruck. All too often, families assembled around a hospital bed is about the other end of life, but here we were at its beginning. Many of us were crying at the joy of it all, so grateful for this miracle of life, so grateful for what could have happened didn't. I know now what "breathtaking" means. It is when something moves you so deeply that you want to speak, but can't because there is no air left in your lungs to make a sound. It's as if God silences us this way because there is nothing we could possibly say that would add to the moment He has created. This was such a moment. With the little air I had left, I could only gasp "Thank you." And we all knew exactly what that meant.

When I find myself feeling God hasn't answered my prayers, I'm reminded He answered this one—that George and Grant both live. He answered the most important prayer of my life, and if He chooses to never answer another prayer as long as I live, it will be just fine because He answered this one. And this one is more than enough for me.

* * * * *

In years to come, close friends of our daughter Jennifer went through similar experiences, but with tragically different results. Their worst "What if" actually happened. Brett and Erin, and then Kelli and Scott, both had their babies die. For Brett and Erin, they knew well in advance their Grace would die once she left the womb, but Erin took Grace to full term anyway. Brett wrote and recorded a beautiful, haunting song for his Grace. He made music in the midst of his sorrow.

Then there was Kelli, who on Wednesday, February 23, 2011, at 7:52 a.m. EST, posted the following on Facebook: "Sweet Baby Ben was born at 8:58 on Tuesday evening with a very weak heartbeat, but no outwardly visible signs of life. He lived for 5 minutes. He weighed 5 pounds, 13 ounces and was 18½ inches long. Everyone commented on what a beautiful baby he is, and we think so as well. Evan absolutely loved meeting his little brother and wanted to 'hold' him as much as possible. We are heartbroken, and we need your prayers more than ever right now."

More than thirteen years have passed since Grant and George's birth, yet I think about it every so often—more than one would normally think given the passage of time. Why did our babies live, while the babies of our daughter's friends die? I don't know. I really don't know.

I'm not a theologian, and I'd prefer to leave matters like this to them, because after all, they need a job. As for why God allows bad things to happen to good people, I don't think we'll ever get that one figured out. I've heard most of the arguments, and some seem more plausible than others. But what I do know for sure is the God who allowed our grandsons to live for over thirteen years now is the same God who allowed Kelli and Scott's son to live just five minutes. He is the same God who allowed Brett and Erin's daughter to breathe her last after only a minute or two. He is the same. And He is good and no less loving to parents He allows to lose their children than He is to those whose babies He allows to live.

One year after Kelli and Scott lost their Sweet Baby Ben, Kelli posted on Facebook a quote she came across by Ralph Fletcher in *Fig Pudding*,

> *"When someone you love dies, you get a big bowl of sadness put down in front of you, steaming hot. You can start eating now, or you can let it cool and eat it bit by bit later on. Either way, you end up eating the whole thing. There's really no way around it."*

And it's not just when someone dies, for we also get a big bowl of sadness when we experience any significant loss and disappointment. Even before the bowl of sadness, some of us also get a big plate of anger appetizers plunked down in front of us that we didn't order. Anger at God for allowing our losses to happen. Anger that life is not turning out the way we think it should. Anger that life isn't fair, and that really bad things happen to really good people.

If we push our plate of anger aside and refuse to eat it, the anger will turn to bitterness we will carry around with us for a very long time. As distasteful as it is, and as many questions as it raises, we need to chew up the anger really well, to a fine powder so we can move on to the next course, the big bowl of sadness. You don't get to the main dish unless you deal with the appetizer first. For many of us though, we'd rather stick with the anger because it numbs us to the big bowl of sadness we don't want to eat.

I know some who get angry at a God who allows innocent babies to die, and then lets the parents live with the loss for the rest of their lives. I know others who offer well-crafted theological explanations for matters of life and death, quoting scriptures touting the sovereignty of God in matters like this. I feel a little uncomfortable when I'm around both types of people.

And it's not just losing babies, either. It was the Fourth of July weekend several years ago when I was mowing our lawn when Janet came out to tell me something that has changed this holiday for us forever. Visibly distraught, she motioned to me to shut off the lawn mower.

"Do you remember the article in yesterday's newspaper about the young woman who was killed in that fiery car crash in Nashotah?"

"Yes."

"It was Stacey Mayer, Steve and Sue's daughter."

"Oh, no. No."

Stacey was 19 years old. We've known her parents for years and babysat for her when she was a toddler. She was such a good girl, so full of life, so full of potential. She's dead and my own young adult children are alive. Why? I don't know. We really don't see much of Steve and Sue anymore, but when we do, we talk a bit about Stacey. Several Christmases ago, Janet and I ran into Sue at the mall, and it wasn't long before we talked about how she and Steve were doing.

"I choose to stay home most days now. I don't get out much. This is the first Christmas we're staying in town since we lost Stacey." A thin film of tears seeped from behind her eyes, exposing the sorrow behind them. "We'll have to get together sometime soon."

"Yeah, that would be great," I said. "We'd love to do this."

We haven't.

I just don't know why God does some of the things He does. I'm okay with this; I don't have to understand everything about God. But I do understand this: even if our worst imaginable "What if" occurs, we can cling to and find hope in "Even if."

"Even if" our babies die, we can trust God will be there for us, and we will make it because we do know He is good. "Even if" we don't understand why God does some of the things he does, He understands exactly what He is doing, and why He is doing it. "Even if" tragedy happens to us, it's not the end of the story. If we choose to have a relationship with God, we'll see our babies and young adult children again on the other side of this life—and this time they will be alive. And when we see them again, they will tell us how they have been even more alive than we've been since the time of our temporary separation many years past.

We so easily forget we live in a fallen world. No advances in the iPhone, flat-screen TVs, or cars powered by electricity are going to make it any better. We still go to war with each other. We still get annoyed with our neighbor when her dog does its business on our lawn. We still get frustrated in navigating through the mine field of voice mail prompts insurance companies use to protect their employees from talking to their customers. It's all part of the fall.

There is something seriously wrong with the world in which we live. The lives we all live now are not what God intended for us. But we as the human race chose to go our own way in the Garden of Eden a long time ago, and we've been suffering the consequences ever since. Why are we surprised tornados strike, people we love get cancer, and that earthquakes shake the foundation of everything? It's part of the system our first parents created for us when they chose not to trust God.

The tragedies of life catch us off guard, because in spite of the mess we've created for ourselves, we still see the goodness of God in so many other ways that we come to expect life will go well for us all the time. We have no problem questioning God when awful things happen, but we rarely question God about all the good things He allows. God gets blamed for an awful lot of things that are not His doing, that have nothing to do with Him. Yet He gets so little credit for all the things He truly is responsible for.

Why don't I have cancer—yet? Why does my husband stay committed me to instead of running off with another woman? Why do I still have a job—for now? Why do my children stay out of trouble—for the time being? Why do I have a roof over my head, clothes on my back, and food in my stomach when much of the world doesn't? Why are all these good things a big part of my life, when they're a hopeless dream for so many others?

Why?

I don't have an answer for these questions. All I know is that God is good, and I cling to this. It is my anchor. It is what gives me hope and what keeps me from going crazy. He is good when life is going well, and He is just as good when everything is not. The goodness of God is not defined or explained by the circumstances in which I find myself. I know every problem I have now, and every difficulty I'll have in the future, are all temporary in the light of eternity.

There's a woman in our church who has been blind since birth; her problem is a temporary one, too. At most, it's a 100-year problem for her, because when she takes her last breath on earth, she'll immediately see very clearly all that is hers in heaven for the rest of eternity.

I also know that even if the worst happens to me here on earth, God will comfort me; He will be compassionate with me. He is the God of all comfort and the father of compassion. We can count on this for sure. Even if the worst happens, God can use it to draw us closer to Himself—if we let Him. He can use it to strengthen us. He may very well make us better people for it. Even if the worst happens, God can use what we go through for greater purposes and reasons than we can ever imagine.

Most of the time, I find all this comforting and encouraging in the midst of my ignorance of why God allows some of the things He does. During the times when I don't draw any encouragement from knowing this about God, it becomes a wake-up call that I don't know God well enough yet to trust Him for all the "What ifs." It's not that He is untrustworthy; it's that it's really hard to trust someone we don't know very well. The "What ifs" of life are God's invitation to get to know Him better. It's often an invitation to a party I'd rather not attend, only to discover when I actually go, how glad I am I did. The "What ifs" remind me I would do well to get to know God better, so the truth of "Even if" becomes more a part of who I am.

Chapter 10

Anger

*If anger were mileage, I'd be a very frequent flyer,
right up there in first class.*
—Gina Barreca

Besides *It's a Wonderful Life*, the Christmas movie about an entire community caring for one of its own, there's another movie I love for the same reason, *Lars and the Real Girl*. It's the story of a single man who lives in a converted garage across the yard from his brother and sister-in-law, Gus and Karen. Lars has a good job, but becomes a recluse after the death of his parents, which greatly concerns Gus and Karen. He is also socially awkward, that is until Bianca comes into his life

Bianca is a life-sized doll Lars ordered online. She has long, dark hair and wears black fishnet stockings. I think you get the picture. Lars takes her everywhere and introduces Bianca as his fiancée, who is a missionary from Brazil. To keep things on the up and up, Lars has her spend each night in a spare bedroom at his brother's house across the driveway. Everyone else in the movie is completely normal.

Lars' brother Gus provides a foil for Lars. He's concerned about his brother becoming more and more withdrawn, and he gets angry at Lars when he uses a life-sized doll to deal with his issues. I won't tell you what those issues are—and I hate that term anyway, but if you watch and listen very carefully to the beginning of the film, you'll figure out what they are. You're smart, I can tell. You're reading this book.

There are several scenes where Gus gets angry at his brother for living in the fantasy world he's created for himself. Gus also gets angry at others for not being as upset as he is about his brother's dysfunctional coping skills. Bianca brings Lars out of himself, and she brings out anger in Gus. But she also brings out the best in the community as it cares for Lars in ways that help him heal and return to real life later in the film. It's a beautiful movie I recommend to anyone who wants to care well for others.

Gus's anger at his brother reveals some interesting dynamics about anger. Like any emotion, anger is a reaction to something. That's all emotions are—reactions. We're wired to react. I cringe sometimes when I hear people advise, "Don't trust your emotions" or "Don't live your life based on your emotions." Comments like this are usually in the context of elevating thoughts over feelings, that somehow living in our thoughts is a better way to live than to live in our feelings.

For me, when I get in trouble, it's usually because of what I think, rather than what I feel. I trust my feelings more than my thoughts. Because when I think about what I'm feeling, I go back to what am I reacting to.

Feelings really aren't the issue, it's what the feelings are trying to tell me about what I am experiencing at the moment. They are like the indicator lights on the dashboard of a car. Those lights tell us how we're doing; do we have enough gas, is the engine temperature okay, are we low on oil? Sometimes those indicator lights tell us it would be a good idea to look under the hood to see what's going on. Emotions are like that, too. They tell us we should take a look at what's going on in our lives causing the reactions we have.

There are two kinds of anger—righteous anger and unrighteous anger. The Bible talks about righteous anger as standing up for what Jesus cares for, and what God holds dear. It's all about God and what's important to Him. We experience righteous anger in response to anything that violates the standards of God. Anger about the sex-slave trade, injustice, child abuse, and other forms of man's inhumanity to man are examples of righteous anger. It's all about God and what He stands for.

Unrighteous anger, however, is all about us. It's all about our needs and expectations not being met. Unrighteous anger is far more common than righteous anger, yet we at times try to explain away our anger as being righteous, when in reality, we are simply trying to justify ourselves.

For me, anger is an unwelcome companion who follows me wherever I go. He's like a stowaway aboard a cruise ship. I'll be going through life quite happy, but then, when I least expect it, anger jumps out in front of me on the promenade deck. It doesn't take much to draw him out of hiding. Calling customer service at my insurance company, returning an item I purchased at a store, trying to get an answer about a computer problem I'm having. Depending on the day, all of these have the potential to evoke my anger. On my better days, I'll think to myself, *"What am I reacting to here?"* With anger, I've learned that what I'm reacting to is something that lurks underneath the shroud of anger. For anger is really a surface emotion that masks other emotions.

In *Lars and the Real Girl,* the anger Gus displays about his brother has its roots in the emotions of fear, hurt, and unmet expectations. I won't tell you how the film depicts this trio of feelings in Gus—I don't want to spoil the movie for you, so I'll talk about me instead. Sometimes when I'm angry, it's really because I'm afraid. My anger is a reaction to something I fear.

On one particular occasion, my wife Janet went out for the evening with her girlfriend, Linnea. As the evening wore on and Janet was yet to return home, I began to feel a bit unsettled. She normally doesn't stay out so late. I started to wonder if something happened. More time passed and my unsettledness grew to anxiety. *Why doesn't she at least call? Was she in a car accident?* Anxiety gave way to fear as more time clicked away on the clock. This had never happened before. Out this late and not calling. Surely she was in a car accident and is lying either in a ditch or a hospital emergency room. Maybe I should start calling hospitals nearby to see if her body is there.

Then I started planning her funeral. *How am I going to help our kids and grandkids deal with this? Where should we have it? Now what were her favorite songs she'd want sung?* She's told me so many times, but I can't remember. I'll ask Linnea to sing, but wait—Linnea is with her and she's probably dead, too. I'll have to find another singer; whom should I ask?

In the midst of my late-night funeral planning. I hear the garage door open and Janet's car pulls in. Within moments, she walks into the house, still smiling over something funny she and Linnea discussed.

I go into a bit of a rant.

"Do you realize what time it is? Where were you? Couldn't you have at least called?"

"We were having such a good time. Time got away from us. I just didn't realize how late it was. I'm sorry," Janet explained.

Humph. I'm still fuming.

OK, so she made a mistake. I get that. But if I get that, why am I still angry?

It was the fear talking.

Fear she had been in a serious accident, or worse yet, had died. We men do not do fear very well, but we've got anger down pat. It's far easier for us to feel anger than to admit our fears. We often gravitate to anger when we are afraid to face our fears. To recognize we're afraid is an admission we are vulnerable, which doesn't sit too well with most of us. To realize we're vulnerable sends us down the path of control. If we can take control of something we fear, then what we fear will be averted. This is how our subconscious often works.

When our kids are little, we control them by keeping them from running into the street because we fear they will run into the path of an oncoming car. That's a good thing. When our kids are in their twenties, we may try to control them because we fear they won't be there to meet our emotional needs. That's a bad thing.

We have anger management classes, but nothing for fear management. There's no *Fear Management for Dummies*. We are all afraid of something. Most of us are more afraid than we care to admit. Even George Bailey was afraid in *It's a Wonderful Life*. When he can't find the money Uncle Billy lost, he gets really angry at Uncle Billy. Unable or unwilling to face his fear that he might end up in jail over the missing money, George's anger escalates when he goes home that Christmas Eve to the people who love him most, his family. He yells at the kids, grouses at Mary, and tells off one of the kids' teachers on the phone. It's a side of George we haven't seen before. But it's all about his fear, and the anger he covers it with, like a black plastic tarp over a pile of rotting leaves left over from last fall.

Gus, in *Lars and the Real Girl*, is angry at his brother for treating his life-sized doll, Bianca, as a real person. His anger covers his fear: What will the neighbors think?

Normal men don't carry around a life-sized doll with them pretending it's a real person. Could this be the beginning of the end for Lars' sanity? Are we going to have him committed? What are people going to think about ME when they realize I have a whack-job for a brother?

To his credit, Gus later learns that by working through his fears, and thus his anger, he helps Lars return to sanity. In fact, the whole community sets aside its fears about Lars' deviant behavior, which ultimately brings about his healing. Which is why I think this is just as wonderful a film as *It's a Wonderful Life*.

* * * * *

In watching my own grandchildren, I've developed a theory about misbehavior in children. I've come to discover that much of the bad behavior in kids is rooted in their fears. I saw this in action when our grandsons George and Grant were about five years old, and were staying with us for the weekend while their parents were out of town.

The boys had been playing well together in an upstairs bedroom when they decided to take their fun downstairs. Grant went first, and as he reached the bottom of the stairs, he called up to George,

"Hey George, bring the tractor down with you."

That's when it all started. The tractor in question was a small metal tractor, very heavy for its size. Rather than carry it down the stairs, George thought it would be more expedient to throw it down the flight of stairs to his brother. I mean, after all, why carry something from point A to point B when you can throw it? This is what five-year-old boys do—they throw things.

George's quick-thinking decision to toss the metal tractor down the stairs never considered the possibility he might make an errant throw. I admire his self-confidence, but he needs to work on his aim, for rather than landing harmlessly on the floor, the tractor missed its mark and grazed off his brother's shoulder.

Grant, our normally affable and laid-back Grant, erupted with anger in such a way you would have thought his arm was just severed, that one eyeball was hanging by a thread from its socket, or he had a mouth full of teeth falling to the floor like last Halloween's dried-out candy corn. With raised fist waving in the air, Grant glared up the stairs and yelled at George about his evil motives, vowing revenge for the calculated and unprovoked attack on him. Pearl Harbor couldn't hold a candle to this offense, or so one might have thought from a toy tractor glancing off a little boy's shoulder. The anger in his eyes looked like a poster from the 1917 Bolshevik Revolution.

George fired back with a barrage of vindictive insults of his own, trying to place the blame on his brother for his own poor judgment. Both of them yelled at each other at the top of their lungs. I was upstairs watching this all unfold in what seemed like slow motion. *What happened*, I wondered? Just seconds before, they had been laughing and playing well with each other.

I sat down on the top stair, grabbed George and his flailing arms, at the same time telling Grant down below to dial it down a few notches. It wasn't the end of the world. It was just a mistake. Gradually, Grant calmed down, but George was still shouting, still visibly distraught, still inconsolable. He then wrestled his arms from my grasp and gave me the tightest hug around my neck a five-year-old can muster.

Sobbing almost uncontrollably, he cried into my ear,

"Please don't tell Mommy. Please. Please don't tell her. Please!"

"Don't worry, George. I won't tell her. Calm down now. You just made a mistake. It's okay; we all make mistakes."

The anger and crying gradually stopped, and George went off to play by himself.

I then went downstairs to talk with Grant. He was still visibly shaken. He had the tendency at his young age to blame other people and other things for anything bad that happened to him. I once watched him yell at a sofa when he was trying to balance himself between it and an easy chair. He accused the sofa of making him fall. We worked on that one for a while. I was a sofa advocate.

In this situation though, another person—his brother George—was indeed at fault, but his reaction was excessive.

What was going through the hearts of these two five-year-old boys that evoked such anger and wrath on both their parts? I had no quick answers and needed time to reflect. With Grant, I explained that his brother was not the evil person he portrayed him as, that he had just made a mistake in throwing the tractor down the stairs. He needed to forgive his brother for simply making a mistake, not for being one of Satan's henchmen.

I then talked to George about admitting his mistake, that Grant could have been hurt a lot worse, and that it was not a good idea to play catch with anyone using heavy metal toys. He got defensive, but soon calmed down.

Within minutes of Mt. Vesuvius erupting in our home, George and Grant were back playing and laughing together, as if nothing had ever happened. This is one thing I like about boys—they can forgive and move on.

But what about the boys' anger? That really stumped me. Why the vicious response by Grant to George's carelessness? Why the fierce hug around my neck from George and the plea not to tell his mother? What was that all about? And how does this incident relate to their other misbehavior?

Maybe the answer came to me in the shower. I don't recall. Most of my good ideas come to me in the shower (and most of the bad ideas while shopping). The best ideas I have always come from God, and I'm pretty sure this was one of them. It occurred to me that Grant's and George's anger was really rooted in their fears.

As a five-year old, Grant had a fear he didn't matter. Added to this was the dynamic that his older brother, by two minutes, always liked to take charge. George preferred to be a leader more than a follower, and liked to be in control. For Grant, this was not nearly as important. Much of the time, he deferred to George. But every now and then, he wanted to be at the head of the line. He wanted to go first. He wanted to be the decision-maker occasionally, rather than his brother. He wanted to be recognized for sometimes being better than his brother.

Even something as simple as sharing toys brought out their fears. When the boys argued over who was going to play with a toy they both wanted, it was about their fear that they would never, never get to play with that toy again the rest of their lives. And if wasn't that fear, then it was Grant's fear he didn't matter, that "my brother is more favored than I am and all the advantages of life will go to him."

So when Grant felt any of this, he fought back to recapture what he feared he lost or would lose. That is what unleashed his anger. He hadn't learned yet that his turn would come. Grant hadn't learned at the age of five how to compromise, how to use his mind instead of his fists to get what he wanted. Nor had he learned the pleasures of delayed gratification. That would come later. All he knew then is that which came so naturally, for him and for many of us—anger.

With George, he had fears, too. Even though he was usually first and the decision-maker, he feared if he capitulated to his brother, even once, he might very well lose first place in line that felt so comfortable to him. His fear in the tractor-throwing incident revealed a different kind of fear than Grant's. It wasn't fear of punishment that brought out his "Please don't tell Mommy." It was his fear of losing his identity and a fear of being alone.

George's passionate hug around my neck after Grant's diatribe came from a place deep in his soul. The place where he was unsure of himself, in spite of all his bluster to hide it. He was afraid that what Grant was saying about him might be true; that he indeed was a bad person. What his twin brother thought of him meant an awful lot to George. He was the one Grant chose to play with. George was the one his brother imitated. He was the one Grant chose to share laughter with.

If what Grant told George in his anger had any truth to it, all such brother bonding could vanish, and if it did, what would George replace it with? Quite a scary prospect for a little five-year-old boy. Scary enough to fight back in anger to defend his personhood, and to protect his relationship with his brother.

Kind of crazy, isn't it? But that is how it is with anger at times. It's something so natural for us to feel, even at a very early age. To feel the fear underlying the anger, however, is a bit scary. We don't like talking about our fears, but somehow, in talking about them, we come to realize they are irrational many times. We confuse what is possible with what is probable. So many of our fears are based on what is possible, while we ignore its probability. It's possible, for example, for the airplane in which we're flying to crash to the ground and kill us. But how probable is it? Not very.

* * * * *

If it's not fear, then it's often sadness or hurt that anger masks. This is where most of my anger comes from. One mild December Saturday afternoon years ago, I was decorating for Christmas by stringing Christmas lights around the outside of our house. I was nearing completion of the job, when Janet came outside and asked if there was anything she could do to help.

"Yeah. Could you go to the hardware store and get an eight-foot extension cord? That's all I'll need to connect the lights to the outlet in the garage." Off Janet went, returning a short time later not with the eight-foot extension cord I needed, but with a six-foot cord instead. When I saw her purchase, I got really irritated.

"A six-foot cord? I told you I needed an eight-foot cord. This won't reach. Didn't you hear me? I said an eight-foot cord."

Added to my harsh words, I piled on facial expressions of disgust, together with lowering my shoulders and letting my arms free fall toward the ground, much like one of the apes in our local zoo. Not a pretty sight. I was clearly not "husband of the year" material at that point. As I continued to grouse, Janet did a very loving thing. In the midst of her righteous irritation with me, she threw the extension cord to the ground, and as she stormed into the house, said, "I am not your mother!"

Whoa. Where is that coming from? Of course, she's not my mother. What does my mother have to do with this? This isn't about my mother. I just wanted an eight-foot extension cord. My mother has nothing to do with this. I continued to fume, trying to figure out how my mother was involved.

Is Janet just crazy, or is there a connection between my anger and my mother? Over the next few hours I started to connect the dots between Mom and my anger that took me to a deep place in my heart. I came to realize my anger at Janet was all about my sadness, hurt, and loss in my relationship with my mother. Janet's getting an extension cord two feet shorter than I needed triggered a theme that plays in the background of my heart, *If you really cared about me you would....* *If you really cared about me, you would have listened to what I asked you for, and would have gotten an eight-foot extension cord rather than a six-foot cord.* I also realized this two-foot error in the extension cord purchase was just a mistake, nothing more. Six-foot cords look a lot like eight-foot cords. Janet didn't wake up that morning thinking what she could do to irritate me. It wasn't intentional that her effort to help me fell two feet short. It was just a mistake and nothing more.

As a child, I didn't feel cared for. I didn't have a voice. I rarely got what I asked for, and I didn't ask for much. That hurts, and it's sad. I could never have verbalized any of this to my parents, for there would have been hell to pay if I did. There was a lot of hitting that went on in my family; I certainly didn't want to invite more of it. My goal as a kid was to hide. To stay out of the way of any anger that would come my way.

One time, my mother was particularly angry at me and slapped me across the side of my head. In doing so, she dislocated one of her fingers, which my dad popped back into place. I have a significant hearing loss in my left ear that an otolaryngologist said could very well have been caused by that blow. I don't get many opportunities to use *otolaryngologist* in a sentence, so I take them whenever I can. I love working *otolaryngologist* into conversations with friends. I also love telling how I came to grips with how my parents raised me. They vindicate themselves in later chapters. Just wait; you'll see.

While anger was front and center in my family growing up, we didn't do hurt and sadness well at all. Most families in the 1950s didn't either. If we weren't worried about polio, then we worried about the Russians dropping a bomb on us. We had no role models for sadness and hurt. No one on *Leave it to Beaver, Father Knows Best*, or *Ozzie and Harriet* was ever sad for longer than three minutes. So if I couldn't feel hurt or sad, and expressions of anger were out of the question, the only thing left was to store all of it like nuclear waste in 55-gallon drums deep down in my soul. The problem with that, of course, is that over time, the toxic waste leaks out, usually at the most inopportune times, like mild Saturday afternoons shortly before Christmas when I'm hanging Christmas tree lights.

"I am not your mother!" jarred me out of myself and started me on a journey of examining where I had come from, how I was processing my past, and how it was harming me in my relationships in the present. It started me down a path of understanding how my anger was about the emptiness and hurt I experienced a long time ago and the sadness that followed.

* * * * *

If anger isn't covering up fear or sadness, then it's most likely hiding unmet expectations. Some expectations are normal and just. I expect my parents will provide for my basic needs. I expect the government will protect me from foreign invasion. I expect my employer to pay me for the services I provide. I expect my spouse to honor her wedding vows and stay faithful to me. All reasonable and normal expectations. There are countless others.

Some expectations are not reasonable, however.

Years ago, when I was in graduate school working on a masters degree in counseling, I came across Albert Ellis, a psychotherapist who developed REBT—Rational Emotive Behavior Therapy. He theorized that people have problems in life, not so much because of their feelings or a dead-beat father, but because they believe irrational thoughts. They believe things that are just not true. Some Christian authors—most of whom never heard of Albert Ellis—talk about believing lies, about replaying tapes in our heads that are lies we've come to believe about God, other people, and ourselves. I prefer irrational thoughts, rather than "lies." Lies imply a degree of intentionality, which isn't always present.

Ellis came up with eleven common irrational thoughts that get people in trouble. His mode of counseling was to show people how foolish they were in believing what they believed. I saw him in action one time in a film clip where he was one of three therapists, each of whom subscribed to three radically different counseling theories. Each separately took turns counseling the same woman with the same problem, using a methodology consistent with their approach to psychotherapy.

When it came to Albert Ellis' turn, he just hammered away at the poor lady, challenging so much of the way she thought and felt as being irrational. He came on pretty hard, I thought. I wondered if part of it was because his parents named him Albert. If my name was Albert, I think I'd have a chip on my shoulder and would come down hard on people, too.

At the end of the film, the narrator asked the lady with the problem to evaluate which of the different therapies she found most helpful. Surprising to me, she gave Albert Ellis really high marks. Many of Ellis' irrational beliefs are rooted in expectations. For example, number one on his hit parade is

It is essential that one be loved or approved
by virtually everyone in his community.

When our expectations to be loved or approved are not met, some of us respond in anger. We'll distance ourselves from those we expect to love us but don't, and eventually we become bitter toward them if our anger is not resolved. Besides distancing and bitterness, passivity will sometimes be the by-product of anger. We may sabotage the plans of others if we're angry with them, as illustrated by what I heard on a missions trip I took to Mali.

In that culture, tribal women are marginalized and expected to bolster the egos of their husbands and feed their pride. Men will invite friends for supper, and how that supper tastes becomes a direct reflection on the husband. If the wife happens to be angry with her spouse, and if she has no voice to express this anger, she will do something to reflect badly on him, like preparing rice poorly on purpose so there will be stones in the rice. When Malians comment "there are stones in the rice," they mean someone is really angry and is being passive-aggressive about it.

There are so many other examples of unmet expectations. Small children show us this very well. I'm angry because I can't have an ice cream cone now (I expect all my desires are to be met now.) I'm angry at my teacher because I didn't get the grade I deserved (I expect all of my efforts will be properly rewarded.) The difference between child anger over unmet expectations and adult anger over the same thing is that we adults are usually better at covering up our anger. But it's there nevertheless.

When my grandson Grant yelled at the sofa for causing him to fall between it and the chair he was straddling, he was angry about the unmet expectation that he should never be hurt when he plays, regardless of his poor decision-making. When I get angry at someone in customer service who can't solve my computer problem, it's because of my expectation that the person on the other end of the line know his or her stuff and cares about me and the inconvenience to me. Unrealistic and unmet expectations.

* * * * *

I am far more angry than I'd like to be. But something I've found very helpful is one small verse in the Bible. It's in Psalm 4:4

> *Don't sin by letting anger control you.*
> *Think about it overnight and remain silent.*

Right after this verse, in some translations, the word *"selah"* appears. People who know a whole lot more about the Bible than I do say the psalms were often meant to be sung, and *"selah"* is a choral direction meaning to pause. To stop for a moment. So here we have the psalmist saying, "Take a lot of time to think about where the anger is coming from, and keep your mouth shut." Then the choral direction is to slow down even more. There's a whole lot of pausing, and thinking, and being quiet going on.

This is all so different from the hydraulic theory of anger that says we need to let our anger out, otherwise the pressure is going to build and build, and we'll eventually explode. If you stuff your anger, it's not going to be pretty. Hit something, smash your fist in a pillow, kick a can, do something physical to release your anger, and you will feel better. The problem with this approach is that it just isn't true.

Psychologists who study this kind of thing tell us that while doing something physical provides temporary relief, it actually leads to more anger, not less of it. Hitting something does nothing to deal with the underlying cause of anger: fear, hurt, or unmet expectations.

The Bible's solution is much more helpful—namely, don't let my anger control me, and instead think about it overnight and remain silent. What I think about during this time is *WHY* I am angry. This is often hard work. It takes time and hearing from God to know what that something is. But I've come to learn that anger is always about something else.

So when angry, I ask myself, "What am I afraid of?" Then, "What am I sad about?" And lastly, "What are my unmet expectations?" Dealing with my fears, hurts, or expectations becomes the task at hand—not the anger. This also helps in dealing with other people who are angry. When I see an angry person, no matter how young or old, I try to look past the anger and think about what he or she might be afraid of, sad about, or what the person's unmet expectations might be. It helps me extend grace to them.

This view of anger also helps me in dealing with conflict. Conflict in which I'm a participant, as well as conflicts where I'm an observer, or as someone brought in to help deal with a conflict. One of the most awful conflicts I ever experienced brought out my anger, as well as hurt, fear, and some unrealistic expectations I held. It was so painful for me that for a long time it was hard to talk about. It's still not easy and I'm reluctant to tell the story even now.

Well, okay. You talked me into it.

Chapter 11

Am I the Lead Actor?

*Most misunderstandings in the world could be avoided if people would
simply take the time to ask, "What else could this mean?"*
— Shannon L. Adler

I am puzzled when people say, "I don't like conflict." Who does?
Who really enjoys the tension and angst that conflict brings? Who
likes sleepless nights brought on by unresolved conflicts?
Who savors those stomach-churning conversations where you have to
discuss hard things you know will upset people? I know as many people
who enjoy conflict as those who enjoy a root canal, colonoscopy, and a
Barry Manilow concert all on the same day. I don't know anyone who
enjoys conflict. Not a soul. But then I don't get out much.

For the three people on our planet who do enjoy conflict, their
enjoyment must come from something else, and conflict just happens to
accompany it. Maybe it's being the center of attention. Or it could be
insecurity, evil, or narcissism. All of these can provide a welcome home
to love of conflict.

For some people, conflict can be a form of manipulation, as in *I'm
putting you on notice not to expect anything from me in this difficult
situation, so you're going to have to handle this one yourself.*

To say "I don't like conflict" is to state the obvious. Other people
are like Neville Chamberlain, prime minister of England during the
1930s, who naively claimed after returning home from negotiating with
Hitler, "We have peace for our time." Now there was a man who really

hated conflict. Many of us are like Chamberlain; we'll do just about anything to avoid conflict.

Business guru Patrick Lencioni says the problem with conflict in most organizations is not that there is too much conflict; it's that there isn't enough of it. Healthy conflict brings issues to the surface that need to be discussed, rather than pretending they don't exist, and thus never get resolved. When processed well, conflict can bring people together, create a bond, and even affection.

One particular conflict I was involved in did just the opposite. It was awful. But I learned a great deal from it that helped me personally. I found a redemptive quality to the conflict, which has helped me immeasurably in caring for others, particularly with missionaries in helping them work through their conflicts,.

So here's the story. It happened in church, of all places. One of the worst experiences of my life happened in church. When I say "church," I don't mean a building. I mean a community of believers in God who stand for what He stands for. Sadly, church is sometimes a breeding ground for conflict.

My particular conflict revolved around a staff person in a church we were attending at the time. We became friends working together in ministry, and he asked me to help him as a volunteer to take on a training position, working side by side with him. All went well, and my role in the ministry began expanding. One of the people on our team, someone I had worked well with, suddenly at one point did an about face. He started to distance himself from me, which was surprising. So I went to him and asked if things were okay between us. They were not.

Ed had a few criticisms of how I was relating with him that made him feel put down by me, especially in a group. This was news to me, as I had no idea I was coming across that way to him. So I apologized, asked for his forgiveness, and committed to working at not doing it again. I thought things were mended between the two of us, but soon the distancing behavior started up again. So I went to Rick, the staff person in charge of our ministry.

"Have you noticed how cool Ed has been? What gives? Do you see me doing things to alienate him?

"Beats me. Yeah, I have noticed. And no, I don't see you doing anything to bug him. In fact, you seem to be walking on eggshells around him. I don't know what's going on with him," said Rick.

Weeks passed.

Then I received an email from Rick asking to meet with me in his office at the church. This was not unusual, for we met occasionally to discuss the training we were doing together. I sat down in his office, and after introductory small talk, Rick hit me with, "The reason I want to meet with you today is that I have gotten complaints from five different people who have a concern about you."

Their "concern" was an accusation that called into question my character and integrity. It came completely out of left field, for I had no idea five of my colleagues so misjudged my motives about my relational style with people.

I was devastated.

After a very long pause, I said, "What they're saying about me isn't true. It's just not true."

"But five people are seeing this in you, and I can't ignore that."

"Yes, but it's not true."

"Well, to be honest, I've noticed the same thing about you myself," Rick said.

I was stunned. Nothing even remotely close to this criticism of me had ever been expressed by him before.

"So here's what I want you to do," Rick said. "I want you to take a year off from ministry, starting right now, and go for counseling to deal with this. Then, after a year, we'll talk again and see where you are at that time."

I went home after the meeting and told Janet what happened. She was shocked and asked, "Well, is it true? How could Rick tell you those things if they weren't true? I mean, if he and five other people think it's true…."

"But it isn't true. I can't imagine what I'm doing to give people that impression."

Being removed from ministry and told to go for counseling was a shock to our systems. We both walked around numb for days. I soon made an appointment with a counselor Rick suggested. Had I been in my right mind at the time, I would have challenged Rick on the need to do this. It was overkill, like cutting off your arm because it itches. Janet then began talking to a few close friends, one by one, about the complaint against me.

"Please be honest with me. Do you see any validity to this criticism of John? Have you ever seen in John what these other people are seeing? Do you have any idea how people could feel about him this way?" Janet asked.

To a person, each one of them was just as surprised as Janet and I were. None of them saw what Rick and the five other people saw. *What's going on here?* I soon got into to see the counselor Rick recommended and told him what happened.

"So how can I help you?" Mike asked.

I told him what the accusation was as I heard it from Rick.

"Is it true?" Mike asked.

"No. It's not. But where I could use help, and why I am here, is to try to discover what I am doing to give the impression that the criticism is true."

"Have you asked Rick about this—about what you might be doing to give this impression?"

"I did, but he wasn't very specific. He said it was just a feeling he was getting. He pointed to a few things that were pretty vague, things that he himself does, and he kept coming back to it's just a sense he has, and that others were feeling the same way."

"This sounds more like an issue between you and Rick. I suggest talking to him more about it. What he describes about your behavior doesn't seem out of the ordinary to me. I think you need to get more specifics from him. I can't really help you until I know more about his concerns."

With that, I thanked Mike and left. When I got back to my office, I called Rick.

"Mike said he thinks this issue is more of a problem between the two of us. He said he can't help me until he knows more specifics about your concern. What can I tell him about the specifics of what you find troubling?

Clearly flustered, Rick stammered a bit. I sensed irritation in his voice as he said, "You need to see someone else then. I want you to see Don instead."

Hmm, I thought. *What am I missing here? I know Rick has high regard for Mike. Why can't he just be more concrete with me?* Poor Mike. I wonder if he'll get anymore referrals from Rick. It never occurred to me to press Rick for concrete examples of what he and the five others were seeing in me.

I made the appointment with Don, and for the next several months, we journeyed down a difficult path together. I brought to him the same issue I brought to Mike, "What am I doing to give the impression to Rick and these five other people that what they think about me is true?"

Don was a masterful counselor. He picked, prodded, and probed, every imaginable aspect of the vague generalities of Rick's criticisms and observations about me. Janet came to several of the sessions, and he did the same with her.

"I've talked to my closest friends," Janet told Don. "Those who know John and me the best, those who have known us for a very long time. I asked them to be brutally honest with me and tell me if they have ever seen John in the same light as Rick and these other five people. Each of them expressed surprise that anyone would have such a criticism of John, because they have never seen anything like it in him themselves."

While this was encouraging to know, it still didn't answer my question of *What am I doing to give people the impression Rick and the five others have of me?* Having examined every possible facet of why Rick would want me to seek counseling, Don and I began to unravel this awful situation. Slowly, over several months, I began to learn I was asking the wrong question. It was like morning fog gradually starting to lift from my eyes, and from my heart. The issue wasn't so much what I was doing, as it was how others were choosing to interpret what I was doing—and how I was responding to the narrative they were espousing. So much of life is asking the right question, and here I had been asking the wrong one.

I see myself and others doing this at times. Several years ago, I started noticing, even in the Bible, how often people ask Jesus a question He completely ignores. Instead of responding to the question, He addresses the heart of the person asking the question. And the heart of the issue was much greater than the question asked. We need to ask better questions of ourselves. Instead of *How can I get what I want?* a better question would be *How can I learn to be content with what I have?* Instead of *Why is this happening to me?* maybe we should ask *How can I grow and mature from this?* Instead of *How can I stay clear of this person who annoys me so much?* maybe we should ask *Why is it so hard for me to cut people some slack?*

The Drama Dynamic

When it comes to interpersonal conflict, one really great question I've learned to ask myself is this, "If my conflict were a play, would I be the lead actor or a supporting actor?"

> *All the world's a stage,*
> *And all the men and women merely players;*
> *They have their exits and their entrances,*
> *And one man in his time plays many parts*
> —William Shakespeare, *As You Like It*

In thinking about conflict as a play, and our role in it, it's always best to start with *Am I the lead actor in the conflict?* It's necessary to be brutally honest with myself and examine whether the drama may be mostly about me, and what I am to learn about myself and others. Is there some flaw of mine being exposed I need to deal with? Am I the source of the conflict? Is my pride showing, like the tops of teenage boys' underwear above their ill-fitting baggy pants? Is the conflict about a poor decision I made and how I'm suffering the consequences? Am I making people miserable to cover up the fact I can't admit to a mistake I made?

Answers to questions like these help determine whether or not we're the stars of the conflict we're in.

Another way we can tell if we're the lead actor is to simply ask God to show us. Just ask. Really, it's not more complicated than this. When we ask questions about our behavior, motives, and attitude, God is more than ready to respond. In fact, I think it encourages Him when we do. I don't think God needs encouragement, unless of course if He's a Chicago Cubs fan, but if He does, this would do the trick. Because if we truly are the lead actors, He'll gently tell us. No finger pointing. No yelling and ranting. No frowns of deep disappointment. Those would be responses from the other guy, the evil one, the Accuser, as the Bible describes him.

God is different. He'll woo us. He'll whisper into our hearts, "Yes, I'm afraid you ARE the lead actor."

Following an appropriate pause, God will say with a smile, "But I know you can do better. You're too good to be behaving and thinking like this. So let's dust yourself off, get back on the saddle, and give it another try. I know you can do this. I'm pulling for you, and I'll be cheering you on from the stands."

Having heard from God, we can then accept responsibility for our failure to love well, and for a whole host of other shortcomings. By acknowledging the ugly truth of who we are at times, we can begin to change, which helps bring out the best in ourselves and other people, rather than the worst.

We need to linger in examining if we truly are the lead actors in the conflict. We shouldn't let ourselves off the hook too quickly. Ask God to shine a spotlight on us so we can see ourselves as we truly are. This is really hard sometimes. Who wants to admit they've been acting like a jerk? I sure don't. I never want to admit that some of the problems I experience are of my own doing. It feels so much better to blame someone else.

Awhile back, I bought a book based solely on its title, *Mistakes were Made (but not by me): Why We Justify Bad Decisions, Foolish Beliefs, and Hurtful Acts* by Carol Tavris and Elliot Aronson. The subtitle describes the book in a nutshell. It's about ignoring the times we are the lead actors in the dramas of life. If we're honest with ourselves and find everything is pointing to us as the lead actors in a conflict, we have a choice to make. We're at center stage with the spotlight on us, so we can choose to do nothing and continue in our lead roles, in which case the conflict will continue and nothing gets resolved. Or we can decide to change. We can face up to our responsibility, admit where we've gone wrong, repent, and ask forgiveness from those we've hurt.

But after all this self-examination, what if we come to the conclusion, *No, I'm not the lead actor*? This will often come if we see that even if we had behaved or felt differently, the conflict would still be there. Dynamics beyond our control fueling the conflict are indications we may not be the lead actors after all.

A good example is in a divorce where children are involved. When Mom and Dad decide to leave each other, a common reaction in children is to feel *"they're splitting up because of me. I must have done something wrong to cause this to happen. If I had behaved better this awful thing wouldn't be happening."*

They're taking on the lead actor role.

It's wrong and we all know it. Childhood comes with a life-is-all-about-me pair of glasses. If things go as they should, children mature and eventually get new life-is-not-just-about-me eyewear. With these new glasses, we learn to see that sometimes we're the lead actors in a conflict, and other times, it's another person.

But if someone else is the lead actor, what is our part? What is our role? What is our responsibility?

It's to be a supporting actor.

If someone else is the lead actor, our role is to be the best supporting actors we can possibly be. It's to be an academy-award-winning-best-supporting actor. It's to be a Robert-DiNero-Sean-Penn-Oscar-winning-supporting actor. It's to be a Katherine Hepburn-Meryl-Streep-type-supporting actress. Being a supporting actor or actress means we're not on center stage. We're in the back or off to the side, letting the spotlight shine on the lead actor, so the focus of the drama of our conflict is on that person, and not us. It's to act in such a way as the true character of the lead actor becomes apparent to careful observers in the audience.

As the theater curtain of the conflict between Rick and me gradually rose, and the fog and smoke on stage began to dissipate, I began to realize our conflict was not so much about me as it was about Rick. He was the lead actor, not me. As one who has gone through life assuming I was the one who was always wrong in any disagreement, this was a startling realization.

"You mean to say this whole mess was more about Rick than me?" I asked.

Really?

But that didn't mean I was off the hook with my share of the responsibility in the conflict. Supporting actors play an important role in any relational conflict. The supporting actor role requires just as much self-examination as the lead actor requires. As actors playing this part, we need to ask ourselves what we are doing to contribute to the conflict. How are we making it worse. How are we hard on people. How are we enabling the lead actor to continue the conflict.

What a relief it was to begin to see my role in the conflict with Rick as a supporting actor in the drama where he was the star, not me. My supporting role wasn't anything I auditioned for, but I did have a responsibility to play the role well. Regrettably, I didn't. I failed on several levels.

To be a really good supporting actress or actor requires us to have not only a high degree of self-awareness, but also some savvy about other people. Up until my conflict with Rick, I thought I knew people pretty well. I have a master's degree in counseling, and 25 years of business experience in a rough industry. To be successful in the business world, I had to learn the difference between what people said and what they meant. I learned what people do is where the truth lies, not in the words they say.

Through many mistakes and reading people incorrectly, I developed a better understanding of people. I became more skilled in telling when people were lying to me. I got better at telling when people had other agendas than what they were projecting. But I fell short in understanding Rick and realizing he was the lead actor and my role was a supporting one. It was a humbling realization.

I realized I was too trusting of him, too naive about his motives, and too willing to ignore important bits of data about his behavior. I was too wrapped up in wanting to belong, to be part of the ministry he led. My need to belong clouded my judgment. I didn't serve him well in my role. I thought he saw me as his friend, but he really didn't. I was a lousy supporting actor, undeserving of a nomination for any of the countless awards the acting profession bestows on itself. My Actors' Equity membership should have been revoked.

As supporting actresses or actors, we have no control over the lead character. None at all. But we do have control over our response to what he or she does. This is the most important part of our role— responding well to the star of the show. That's where I blew it. I responded poorly to two significant events that occurred with Rick before our conflict. One was how he handled the situation with our mutual colleague, Ed. The other was what he told me about a change in title for him at the church.

In the first situation, I went to Rick about a complaint Ed had against me. I thought the complaint was totally unwarranted, but wanted to check it out with Rick. He thought the criticism unjustified and told me not to give it a second thought. So I didn't, which was a big mistake. I should have asked him to meet with Ed and me so the three of us could deal with the issue and put it to rest, one way or the other. Rick, however, did nothing. This was the first clue I ignored—that he was not the friend I thought he was.

Nor was Rick the leader I hoped him to be. A good leader, when he senses tension between people on his team, brings people together for the sake of the team, to talk about complaints they have against each other. Otherwise, fertile soil develops for roots of gossip to germinate, which is what later happened. It wasn't helping my critics to harbor ill-will against me and not be challenged by Rick to reconcile with me over perceived grievances they had.

The second incident with Rick I mishandled occurred when he told me about his desire to be named Associate Pastor. At that point, he was on staff as a paid ministry "director," doing all the work of an associate pastor, but without the title. Visibly agitated at one point, he nervously said, "I don't know what I'm going to do if they don't give me the 'Pastor' title. I'm doing all the work of a pastor. I don't understand why it's taken so long to get this. I spoke to the senior pastor six months ago. He told me to be patient and that the new designation was in the works."

I cringed inside.

What a display of ego, I thought. *What difference does your title make? You'll still be doing the same work at the same pay and have the same power.* I wanted to ask, "Why is the title so important to you? I can understand you being disappointed, but your reaction goes beyond disappointment—it seems excessive to me."

Instead, I said nothing. I ignored this big, dangerous, red flag waving in front of me. I chose to let this incident pass because I had a good thing going in the ministry in which both of us worked. Life was going really well, and I think I chose to remain silent because I belonged to something larger than myself. I didn't want to jeopardize anything. And after all, I don't like conflict. But in keeping silent, I failed my friend Rick.

In the months that passed, the training program I taught with Rick in our church began to take off. We had lots of people taking the class, and Rick began turning more of it over to me. I redesigned the curriculum, brought in outside speakers, and increasingly, was becoming the face of the training. Rick's absence from the once-a-week-class began to increase as he had schedule conflicts with his wife, requiring him to stay home to watch their kids while she was gone.

People began coming to me with questions rather than to him. Once someone came to me with a criticism of Rick, wanting me to do something about her criticism.

"Have you talked to Rick about your concerns?" I responded.

"Well, no."

"I think you should. If you don't get anywhere with him, come back to me and we'll go see him together." Right out of Matthew 18 and what Jesus said about handling complaints we have against someone. I wish Rick would have returned the favor when the "five people" came to him with complaints against me. He didn't. Instead he separated me from my critics.

The Matthew 18 approach in the Bible works a whole lot better:

If another believer sins against you, go privately and point out the offense. If the other person listens and confesses it, you have won that person back. But if you are unsuccessful, take one or two others with you and go back again, so that everything you say may be confirmed by two or three witnesses. (Matthew 18:15-16)

Some would argue this passage only applies to "if another believer sins against you." Isn't failing to love someone a sin? I think it is.

But even if we take Matthew 18 off the table, how can we ignore what the Apostle Paul says in his letter to the Galatians?

Dear brothers and sisters, if another believer is overcome by some sin, you who are godly should gently and humbly help that person back onto the right path. And be careful not to fall into the same temptation yourself. Share each other's burdens, and in this way obey the law of Christ. If you think you are too important to help someone, you are only fooling yourself. You are not that important. (Galatians 6:1-3)

When you separate critics from those they criticize, bad things happen. Gossip, slander, and bitterness—to name a few. I was naive not to ask Rick for an audience with my accusers and for him to mediate such a meeting. Instead, I assumed he was on my side, I assumed he believed in me, and I assumed his heart was in the right place. I assumed he knew I didn't want his job, and that I saw my role as doing the best I could to support him, to help him be as successful as he could be. That's what friends do for each other. But as someone once said, "Assumption is the lowest form of communication, followed closely by e-mail."

I saw this dynamic played out with a missionary couple who came to Janet and me for help in processing a conflict they had on the mission field. There was so much tension and gossip going around among their missionary community that it became untenable for the couple to continue on with this team. When I asked the husband what he wished he would have done differently, he paused and said he couldn't think of anything. Ninety percent of what he did I wholeheartedly concurred with. He did what I would have advised others to do in a similar situation—with one exception. With ten percent of his story. That ten percent usually does us in, the ten percent that trumps the ninety percent of what we do right.

"Joe, the only thing I see you could have done differently would be in response to your field director in the conversation you had with him before you headed back to field from your home assignment. His comment to you, 'Joe, some of your colleagues have come to us recently and said you were being divisive in implementing the new policy we developed. But we're going to send you back anyway' was a turning point."

"How so?"

"When he told you that, you didn't say anything, right?"

"Yes, that's right. I didn't say anything because I had dealt with this back on the field months earlier. I heard the same rumor and went to each of the people on our team and asked them if I had come across as being divisive with them. I did so because if I was, I wanted to apologize and ask for their forgiveness. They all said, 'No, not at all. We don't see you being divisive with us.'"

"Yeah, I can understand why you didn't say anything, but you were naive."

I understand why Joe didn't say anything because I made the very same mistake several years earlier when Rick told me, "five people have come to me expressing concern over you." What went though my mind at the time was *what am I doing to give people this impression?* For Joe, what was going though his mind was *I've already dealt with this; it's no longer an issue.* We were both naive. The ten percent mistake came back to bite us both.

"How was I naive?" Joe asked.

"You were naive because you trusted this problem had gone away, when it really hadn't. You trusted your field director and you trusted your colleagues. But someone was not being honest with you. Either your field director was messing with the truth, or your teammates on the field were lying."

"Well, what should I have done then?" asked Joe.

"I would have said to your field director something like the following in as calm and gentle a manner as possible:

"'Wow. That is a serious charge—my being divisive. I thought I addressed this issue with my colleagues. They said I wasn't divisive. But if I am, that's sin and should be dealt with. So before we go any further, I need to know who is telling you this so I can go to them and repent. I honestly don't see it in myself, so I'm going to need some help here to point specifically to what I've said and done to warrant this accusation. I certainly don't want to be divisive, so I need the input of others so I can change. If the people who are telling you this are the same people I spoke to, we'll need your presence in the meeting to get to the truth. Because what you just told me contradicts what they said to my face.'"

Nothing good happens when people being criticized are separated from their critics. It's quite possible something else is going on here. The field director may have been lying. Sometimes leaders even in Christian organizations lie. A more likely possibility is that these rumors were still surfacing, in spite of what Joe did to quell them, and the field director was either unskilled in dealing with the issue, or else had too many other pressing things on his plate at the moment. Nevertheless, bringing everyone together to get at the truth would have helped a great deal. But sometimes parties in a conflict have a vested interest in not getting at the truth. I think this was the case with my conflict with Rick, by now "Pastor Rick."

After months of meeting with Don the counselor, I called Rick and asked, "The people who came to you with the accusations against me, who are they?"

"I can't give those names out. Why do you ask?" Rick wanted to know.

"Because if I've sinned against them, I need to go to them and ask for their forgiveness."

Becoming agitated on the phone and raising his voice, he said again, "I can't give out the names of the three people who came to me."

"Sure you can. It would be the biblical thing to do. How can I change if I don't talk to the people I've offended?" I replied.

"They'll just tell you exactly what I told you earlier."

"I need to talk to them myself," I said.

With great reluctance, he gave me the names of three people. Another red flag went up, because months earlier, he had been quite specific to say five people had come to him. But now we're down to three. Over the next week, I contacted two of the three and met with them separately in person. They both expressed surprise when I told them the concerns Rick said they each had brought to him about me.

"No, I didn't say that at all to Rick. I don't know why he said I did," said one.

"I can't imagine why he would tell you I said that because I didn't," said the other.

Both people were mutual friends of mine and Rick's. They had no ax to grind either way. I knew they were telling me the truth. If they had said those things to Rick, I know they would have told me so. Because of their character and integrity, I'm also convinced they would have come to me first with any concerns they had about me.

The third person—a woman—was out of town, so I called her. In an unrelated incident in the past, she admitted she had gossiped about me to Rick concerning another matter that turned out to be untrue. She never apologized for it, either. When I asked her about the most recent incident, she denied bringing any complaints to Rick. So what started with five people going to Rick with accusations about me dwindled to just Rick himself having a concern. When I talked with the three "accusers," I did so without them knowing I was talking to the other two. Either the three of them were together untruthful with me, or Rick was. It was obvious to me. Rick was the one who was untruthful.

Why?

It's because the Diotrephes Syndrome was at work.

Chapter 12

The Diotrephes Syndrome

Pride is the chalice into which all human sins are poured: it glitters and jingles and its arabesque lures your gaze, while your lips involuntarily touch the seductive beverage.
—Vladimir Odoevsky

After meeting with my counselor Don for several months, I began to wonder what was going on with Rick that he would lie to me. Data I had previously ignored about him and didn't understand at the time, soon began to make sense. When I thought things were mended with Ed, only to later discover he was still distancing himself from me, it should have given me pause as to why Rick was not doing anything about it.

Because when I talked to Rick, his "I don't know what's going on with him" comment was inadequate. My response wasn't any better; I just shrugged my shoulders. I made the same mistake my missionary friend Joe did when his field director told him, "Some of your colleagues are telling us you're being a bit divisive." He ignored the comment, just as I ignored Rick's.

As I suggested to Joe, I should have said something to Rick like, "I think we need to get to the bottom of this. It seemed like Ed and I were reconciled, yet now he's back to distancing himself from me. We used to be friends, but something has changed. Can the three of us meet so we can resolve this mystery? It would be good for our relationship, and good for our ministry team."

Rick could have mediated the conversation to get to the root of the matter. It seems odd he would not have suggested this on his own. He was always very good with people, and very skilled in reading between the lines. One of the things I liked about him was his sensitivity to relationships. He was very relational, so his silence on this issue was out of character. But as odd as his response to this issue was, even more puzzling was his remark to me I mentioned earlier, *I don't know what I'm going to do if I'm not named "Pastor."*

His comment and his distress about it both surprised and disturbed me, like a bad bowl of Grandma's chili she enters each year at the state fair. This was not like Rick. So out of character.

Or was it?

Counseling with Don was very helpful to me. I know some people, usually those in the church, who don't have much use for counselors. The problem with counseling is there is so much bad counseling going on. There are several landmark studies that found about half of all counseling actually makes things worse for people, and no counseling is many times better than any counseling at all. One pastor, for example, told me with smugness in his voice, his philosophy of counseling is "Jesus is the answer. Now tell me your problem."

You can't make this stuff up; it's really what he said. Honest.

Having received referrals from Rick before, Don knew him and the church where he served. He told me there were other things going on with Rick, and other people in my story I didn't know about, but which he had to keep confidential. The one thing he did tell me was that Ed, the colleague upset at me, was also gossiping about others in our ministry. This led to his removal from leadership, which led to him leaving the church.

Near the end of my time with Don, I went to meet with Rick. I took Janet with me, for we both wanted to reconcile with him. Before reconciliation though, I had to forgive. In theory, forgiveness isn't rocket science, but in practice, it's like going to Mars.

The Bible is quite clear about forgiveness. It's choosing to relinquish my rights to make someone pay for the offense he or she has committed against me. Forgive and forget? No, no. It's not about forgetting what someone did. It's being fully aware of what the other person did, the harm it caused, and the implications of that harm.

You can't reconcile without forgiveness, but you can forgive without reconciliation. For while forgiveness requires only one participant, it takes two to reconcile—just like the tango. For many months, when Janet and I saw Rick at church, it made our stomachs churn. Especially Sunday mornings when he was at the pulpit making announcements. We both knew we needed to forgive, but it was hard.

Forgiveness is not something you can bring about by just gritting your teeth and trying harder. Forgiveness starts with wanting to, and then waiting and praying your want-to opens your heart. To release the offense, to be done with it. This is a supernatural act.

Only God can change our hearts. He is the one who gives us the strength and power to forgive, to let it go, to release the other person from the justice he or she deserves. It doesn't matter how other people respond to my forgiveness; they might not even know I've forgiven them. They might not even think they need forgiving. None of this matters. The only thing that matters is what I do. That I forgive.

Reconciliation is another matter.

When I entered Rick's office, he looked surprised that Janet was with me. He tried to ease the tension with small talk. I was polite, but cut short the chit-chat.

"Rick, the reason we're here is because Janet and I want to put closure on what happened over these last months. I want to report back to you what I've learned in the time I've been counseling with Don. I learned my contribution to the problem is that when Ed first complained about me, I didn't speak up and try to address those complaints by getting you involved. My failure to do so allowed things to spiral out of control. I'm really sorry about this and I hope you will forgive me. This whole situation taught me a great deal, and I can assure you I'm committed to not letting something like this happen again. But if it did, I would make every effort to address issues that come up, not assume things are okay when they really aren't.

"So that is what I've learned is my part, and I take ownership of it.

"Your contribution to the problem is different. You originally told me five people came to you with the same complaint about me. But in a subsequent conversation, your story changed and it became three people, not five. When I asked you the names of the three people, you were reluctant to give them to me. I can see why. I met with two of the three in person, and each one of them denied ever bringing any concern about me to you. They told me they did not say what you told me they said. The last of the three I spoke to on the phone, and she said the same thing.

"So it comes down to the fact you lied to me."

"But what about my own concern with the things I mentioned to you?" Rick interjected.

"I asked you about those on several occasions and you were never specific with me. It was always 'it's just a feeling I have about you.'

"Your lying to me about five, then three people, was quite damaging to both me and Janet. Basing your actions on 'it's just a feeling I have about you' caused us a lot of pain."

Janet began to tear up. Rick was a cold statue.

"But over the last several months, I have come to forgive you for what you've done. I would like to somehow be reconciled with you over this, but for that to happen, I'm going to need a few things from you. I need you to first recognize your sin and the deep hurt and needless pain you caused both Janet and me. I need you to understand the toll your lies have taken on us. And I need you to admit you indeed did lie to me, and to be remorseful about it. And finally, I would like you to commit to working at never repeating this type of behavior again with me."

He sat there stone silent, never blinking.

Rick broke the silence with, "I can't do that. I still stick to my story." Interesting choice of words, *I still stick to my story*. People confident they're telling the truth don't talk like this. People backed into a corner do.

"I'm sorry to hear that," I responded. "I hope you change your mind, and if you do, please call me."

With that, Rick got up from his chair, and as if nothing ever happened, put his pastor face back on, and with a big smile, ushered us out of his office, asking, "Now, how are those little kids of yours doing? They sure must bring you both a lot of joy."

Over time, the pain of the entire experience lessened. God confirmed to me in several different ways that Rick's original accusation about me was not true, that his *it's just a feeling I have* was about him, and not about me. He was the lead actor; I was the supporting actor.

For years, I didn't understand the "why" of all this. Why did he make up this complaint about me? Why did he lie to me? I thought we were friends. I had never done anything to hurt him. I thought we were on the same team working together. It didn't make any sense at all.

One of the advantages of getting older is often over time things that didn't make sense earlier in life will sometimes become quite clear and explicable later. It seems the further removed we are from puzzling situations, particularly in relationships that sour, the easier it becomes to make sense of what never made sense before. Such was the case with Rick. Here is how it happened.

One day, I was reading a passage of scripture near the end of the Bible, III John, a very brief letter of only fourteen verses. Not much of a letter as far as quantity goes, more like a large Post-it note. But what God spoke to me through these fourteen verses suddenly put my Rick experience into a perspective that made perfect sense. It was like all the squares in a Rubik's cube coming together, where all the colors match in each row and column.

The apostle John wrote this letter near the end of his life to his friend Gaius. He commends Gaius for walking in the truth, as John heard about Gaius' virtuous character from others. John goes on to praise Gaius for caring for "the brothers," or "traveling teachers," as some versions describe them. Most scholars feel these were early missionaries of the church. John encourages Gaius to keep on keeping on in his care of them.

Then something really odd happens.

John abruptly changes the warm tone of his Post-it-note-sized letter, and talks about someone else in verse 9, a character named Diotrephes.

> *"I wrote to the church, but Diotrephes, who loves to be first, will have nothing to do with us."* (NIV)

Not much is known about Diotrephes, except that scholars think he was a high-ranking official of the early church, possibly even a bishop. So here we have a leading church official who will have nothing to do with the Apostle John. Had there been phone calls and voice mail in those days, Diotrephes would not have returned them. Had there been texting or email, he would not have responded. Interesting. One of the inner circle of Jesus' apostles, John is described as the one whom Jesus loved. And yet Diotrephes will have nothing to do with him? I mean, we're talking rock star caliber disciple here. The Michael Jackson, Beatles, and Bono of apostles—and Diotrephes will have nothing to do with him? What gives with that?

John tells Gaius that Diotrephes is gossiping maliciously about *us*. Us?

John switches from first person singular to first person plural. Who is the other part of us?

It's Gaius, recipient of John's letter.

That being the case, what could the malicious gossip be about? From the context we see, it probably has something to do with caring for the traveling teachers, the early church missionaries. Gaius developed a reputation of caring for people, the apostle John applauds him for it, and for this, a high-ranking church official spreads malicious gossip. Hmm.

This is starting to sound familiar.

Not only will Diotrephes have nothing to do with the Apostle John—and most likely Gaius, the other party who makes an "us," but he also wants nothing to do with the "brothers," the traveling missionaries. Moreover, the text says anyone who does care for these Christian workers, "he puts them out of the church." Since Gaius is commended for his care of these traveling teachers, we can logically infer Gaius was one of those kicked out of the church by Diotrephes.

This is now really sounding familiar.

I wonder if Rick noticed when people started coming to me more than to him during the training class we taught together. I never gave it a second thought at the time because it didn't mean anything to me. Since he was taking more time off from the class due to family commitments, I was just more available. I also wonder if he was troubled by how the class just grew and grew. By the time I stopped teaching with him, the class size had doubled, partly because I actively recruited people to take the class. I promoted it a great deal more than he did.

The other piece that tied the Diotrephes story together with mine was how the Apostle John described Diotrephes as one "who loved to be first." What an interesting expression, *one who loved to be first.*

Some Bible translations render it "who loves to be the leader." There's nothing wrong with wanting to be the leader, but to love it? Yes, there's something definitely wrong when a person loves to be first. John knew this only too well, because as a young man, he had been guilty of the same sin. He too loved to be first.

Mark 10:35-45 and Matthew 20:20-28 record the story of John and his brother James, along with their mother, who go to Jesus and ask if one of them could be on the right of Jesus and the other on his left in eternity. The remaining ten apostles, as you can imagine, were indignant. It's here that Jesus teaches the first will become last and the last will become first. This hard truth must have stuck with John, for as a much older man, he saw a little of himself from his youth in Diotrephes, the church leader who loved to be first. It takes one to know one.

The first time I came across this little-known and little-preached-about passage concerning Gaius and Diotrephes, it brought me back to the time when I was in Rick's office and he confided in me, "I don't know what I'm going to do if they don't name me 'Pastor.'" The cringe I felt inside of me then was the same feeling I felt when I read this Bible passage.

There's something wrong with anyone who loves to be first or who says, "I don't know what I'm going to do if they don't name me 'Pastor.'" Both statements reveal pride, like a piece of spinach caught between one's teeth. Church leaders who carve out a niche for themselves to fill an ego need can easily feel threatened.

When you love to be first, everyone is a threat.

This was why Diotrephes took out Gaius, and John the Apostle as well. They were a threat. The odd thing is that Diotrephes and Gaius were polar opposites in their positions in the community. Diotrephes as a high-ranking church leader would have been very visible and an out-front kind of guy. Gaius, on the other hand, was a behind-the-scenes character. Caring well for people is almost always done behind the scenes, just as Gaius cared for the traveling missionaries. Caring for others doesn't win anyone many kudos or acclaim. It's most often done one-on-one without drawing attention to itself. Yet Diotrephes felt threatened.

Some leaders I've met and followed have been the most relational and caring people I have ever known. There is a certain type of leader, however, who lacks warmth and people skills, and who is easily intimidated by others with more relational qualities. Such leaders are often intimidated by those more caring than they are.

In working with Rick, I didn't need to be upfront. I was happy just being his sidekick. I didn't need to prove anything to anyone. Nothing to prove, nothing to lose. I knew who I was, and I was comfortable in my own skin. I didn't need any power or control. I had all I wanted. Rick, on the other hand, I think needed more; he needed to be named Pastor. And that is the scary part—when we *need* recognition or a new title. Something's wrong when this happens, and this something is pride.

Dennis D. Morgan, in his book *Fighting for Peace—Combating Conflict with Character,* makes a strong case for his premise that all conflict is caused by an abundance of pride and a lack of humility. Just one point to the whole book. I love it. An abundance of pride and a lack of humility are the root of most conflict. Morgan supports his thesis with many examples from the Bible.

I saw a great example of this on a mission trip I took to Tajikistan, one of the former Soviet republics in Central Asia. The mission pastor at our church asked me to come with him to help put on seminars for young church pastors with little or no theological training. He was to teach on church leadership, I was to teach pastoral care skills.

When we weren't teaching we were meeting with people and participating in the life of the community. One afternoon, we sat in on a meeting of most of the pastors in the area. They wanted to form a ministerial association, but had difficulty getting it off the ground because they couldn't agree on two issues: at what church would the meetings be held, and secondly, who would be the "president" of this fledgling group.

They all wanted the group to meet in their particular church, and they all wanted to be "president." They all loved to be first, and they were all firmly enmeshed in *I don't know what I'll do if I'm not named "Pastor"* thinking. Leadership and being first became too important to these men. It troubled them greatly that the group would meet somewhere besides their church, and that someone besides them might be the leader. This dynamic led to the ministerial association never forming. They just couldn't get past their own pride.

A missionary friend of ours who travels the world told me recently about a trip he made to Nepal, "Pastors there don't have material goods, so they make up for it by fighting for control...it's all ego." All of this illustrates a related principle to pride, and it goes like this:

That which bothers us the most often reveals the idols in our life.

This is so closely related to pride, it's hard to see. But if we start with, "Why am I so bothered by this? Why is this so important to me?" the answer will be often be found at the end of the path leading to our own pride.

Another story that comes to mind illustrating this point is the thorn in the flesh passage Paul the Apostle writes about in his letter to the church in Corinth.

> *... even though I have received such wonderful revelations from God. So to keep me from becoming proud, I was given a thorn in my flesh, a messenger from Satan to torment me and keep me from becoming proud.*

Three different times I begged the Lord to take it away.
Each time he said, "My grace is all you need. My power works
best in weakness." So now I am glad to boast about my
weaknesses, so that the power of Christ can work through me.
That's why I take pleasure in my weaknesses, and in the insults,
hardships, persecutions, and troubles that I suffer for Christ.
For when I am weak, then I am strong. (2 Corinthians 12:7-10)

People often go to this passage to talk about pain and suffering, but I wonder if the main point is really more about pride. We work so hard to become first. We work so hard to overcome our weaknesses, to prove something to someone—even someone who may be dead. Maybe instead of fleeing from our weaknesses or working so hard to minimize them, we should embrace them. When we embrace our weakness, it gives God room to maneuver in our lives. It gives Him a chance to make us better than we are in ways that bring Him glory, and not us.

It's much easier to see all this in someone else than it is to see it in ourselves. I think God sometimes places dysfunctional people in our lives as gentle reminders that we could easily be just like them, and at times we already are, but don't know it. It raises the question, though, how are we to deal with the controlling, prideful people in our lives, like those who love to be first? As someone who deals with my own pride all the time, don't look at me for the answer. I see pride raising its ugly head in me more than I'm willing to admit. But somehow I think the solution to pride must start with forgiveness.

Chapter 13

Forgiveness

Be kind, for everyone you meet is fighting a great battle.
—Philo of Alexandria

My mother was an angry person. She had many things to be angry about. Falling for my birth father and getting pregnant with me, being one. Then there was Harry, my stepfather, who often spent more time with his friends at the local tavern than with her. While he was very gregarious and fun-loving, she was more of an introvert and homebody. At her core, I think my mother was angry at herself and the mistakes she made. As so often the case with unresolved anger, she lashed out at people close to her who had nothing to do with the source of her anger.

My dad would get angry, too, particularly if he had been drinking. I spent a big chunk of my childhood trying to stay away from both of them. They scared me. But it was hard staying away from them in a 1,400 square foot ranch house shared by five kids and their two parents.

A lifesaver for me was a bedroom my dad built for my brother Joe and me in the basement. I loved it down there. It was where I could hide. Always cool in the summer, it was my man cave—long before man caves were invented, and long before I was a man. It was my boy cave.

Until I was sixteen, I hated summers and school vacations. One rainy Saturday afternoon, I watched an old James Cagney movie on television where he played a prison inmate marking time until his release by drawing a big X through each day that passed on his calendar. I thought this was a good idea, so I did the same thing. Each big X marked one less day I had to be at home, and one day closer to when I could return to the safety of school.

During school vacation, I had greater exposure to danger in the house. Dad worked second shift, which meant he'd be home in the mornings, not leaving for work until about 2:30 p.m. So I had to find ways to stay away from him. This was especially challenging when he was on vacation. We never did much during his vacation, rarely taking any trips. It always seemed like we didn't have enough money.

One year, my mother made shirts for me to wear to school. You could tell they were homemade. I had two of them and rotated the shirts during the course of the week. Another time, my tennis shoes wore out and I asked for a new pair. That got them upset. I didn't think I was ever going to get new shoes, until one day they came home from shopping, and my dad walked through the door and threw a new pair of tennis shoes at my feet in disgust. Fortunately they fit.

It always felt like my parents were unhappy with me. It's the lens through which I viewed my childhood. One significant event of my unhappy childhood happened when I watched a 1938 movie on TV about Father Flanagan's Boys' Town, starring Spencer Tracy and Mickey Rooney. It was about a home in Nebraska for delinquent boys.

Several weeks after watching the movie, I noticed my parents getting mail from Father Flanagan's Boys' Town, which made me wonder if they were going to send me there. The mail kept coming over a period of several months and I was sure I was headed to Nebraska because I was so bad. I never got in trouble with the law, and my parents never got a call from school about my behavior or grades. I didn't know what I was doing that got them so angry at me. I didn't want to move to Nebraska, so I tried extra hard to be good, but it seemed like I was never good enough.

One Christmas, our whole family was in the kitchen and my dad wanted us all to sing a Christmas carol. I couldn't. It wasn't that I didn't want to, but I just couldn't. I froze and then he got mad, and the madder he got, the more frozen I became. Then I started crying at his anger, which disgusted him, so he made me stand outside in our attached garage where I shivered. I thought that was the last straw, and the day after Christmas, I'd be on the first bus out of town to Boys' Town, Nebraska.

It wasn't until I was much older that I realized the mail they got from Father Flanagan's Boys' Town was most likely a direct mail fund-raising piece. They probably sent in a contribution, which triggered more mail. That's my guess, and if my parents were still alive, I would ask them about this.

Things changed for the better when I turned sixteen. I got a job at a restaurant and convenience store. I worked as a cook, and because I was one of the few teenage boys who could crack open an egg and fry it without breaking the yolk, I got to work Saturday and Sunday mornings. It was a great shift because it wasn't nearly as busy as the night shifts I worked during the week. I also enjoyed working Saturdays and Sundays more because I wasn't so tired then.

I remember being very tired in high school. I worked about thirty-five hours a week most weeks, except during basketball season, where I sat on the bench for three of the four years I was on the team. During basketball season I only worked Saturday and Sunday mornings, but during the off-season, I worked every weeknight except one. I would get home about 11:30 p.m. each night, and was just exhausted the next day. On my off night, I would go to bed around 7 p.m. I was so tired.

The only time I ever got in trouble in high school was when I fell asleep in US History. The teacher thought I was being disrespectful so he sent me to the office, but I was just tired. When I told the vice-principal what happened, he just nodded and told me to stay in the office until my next class. Nothing else happened. Maybe he knew what it was like to work long hours and then fall asleep in US History.

The great thing about my job was that it got me out of the house and allowed me to save money for college. I also started buying my own clothes. I did everything I could to avoid being home, and getting a job really helped. During those years, when I started to think about what I wanted to do with my life, I decided I wanted to work in a school building. For me, school buildings were places of safety. No one would yell at me at school, and no one would hit me there either. I knew custodians didn't make much money, so I decided to become a teacher, because they made more money, and because they got to work in a safe place where hitting was not allowed.

With the money I saved from my job, I thought all I could afford was to attend a local university as a commuter student. I'd still have to live at home, but I could find ways to spend as little time there as possible. I was resigned to do this, until one day at school, someone cared for me by listening really well and probing with a few insightful questions that changed the direction of my life. You can read more about this in the last chapter, unless of course, you think now is about the right time to sell this book at your garage sale for twenty-five cents.

My plans changed and I was able to afford to go away to college, the only one in my family to have done so at that time. Among other things, four years away at college taught me the power of forgiveness. Because it was during those four years I learned more about Jesus and how he wants us to live. He's all about forgiveness. My home, which used to be dangerous because of the people in it, was no longer frightening.

Forgiving my parents released the power they had over me, and it released me to be a more compassionate and understanding person. Forgiveness begins with knowing what we're forgiving someone for. I wince sometimes when I see on TV loved ones of someone killed within the past twenty-four hours proclaim they forgive the person who ended the life of a person dear to them. It takes time for loss to sink in, and people can't possibly know the depth of their loss within a few hours. This kind of forgiveness is drive-through, fast-food forgiveness. Satisfying for the moment perhaps, but not so much for the long term.

When our grandkids get in a spat with each other, their parents taught them to say they are sorry and then ask their sibling for forgiveness. When this happens at our house, we'll say, "… and what exactly are you sorry for?" Often they don't know, and often the only thing they're sorry for is getting caught. These events provide great learning opportunities.

When we hear people actually name what they have done to harm us, it makes forgiving them a lot easier. We know then that they know what they've done to us. Sometimes though, people don't come to us to ask for forgiveness. Sometimes they never admit how they've wronged us. This makes forgiving them harder, but no less important. Forgiveness can be difficult. We can try really, really, hard on our own strength to forgive, but ultimately, it takes spiritual power to pull it off.

For me, it was easy to know what to forgive my parents for. The physical and verbal abuse I received from them, along with the neglect, are things no child should ever experience. I don't think of the neglect very often, because for a long time, it seemed normal to me. As a child, the only time I seemed part of my parents' life was when we'd go visit their friends on Sunday afternoons. We did a lot of that growing up— either going to someone's house, or having another family come over to our house. All of my parents' friends had children my age, or the ages of my brother and sisters. That's one pleasant thing I remember enjoying about my childhood.

Growing up, I felt like a nuisance and inconvenience to my parents. After learning my father adopted me when I was five, I thought maybe he wished he hadn't. Maybe that's why I was never part of his life. One thing I remember him doing was coming to watch a football practice when I was a sophomore. I played quarterback and one day after practice, I saw him near the stands. It must have been one of the days he was on vacation. He offered advice on how I could do better, that's all I remember. But I don't remember him ever coming to watch me play in a game. That's when I noticed the neglect, because other players had their parents come.

This especially hurt when I was in eleventh and twelfth grade playing basketball and "Parents' Night" was on the schedule. Players would be introduced at half-time and their parents would come down from the bleachers to stand next to their sons at mid-court. My parents never came. It was usually me and maybe one other player who did not have a parent show up. That is when I noticed this wasn't normal. Seeing all those other parents standing next to their sons, with me standing alone, looking for a hole to crawl into. I explained it away saying my dad worked second shift and couldn't get off work, and my mother didn't drive and so she couldn't make it. I knew though, my dad could have used one day of his six weeks of vacation to come, or my mom could have gotten a ride from one of our neighbors.

I never said anything to my parents about this. I don't think they realized how important it was to me for them to be there. Sometimes people with difficult childhoods will go back as adults to confront their parents with how they harmed or neglected them. Using lots of "I" statements is how the drill goes.

"I felt scared when you…

"I was so angry when you …

"The time you _____ I felt devalued, like I didn't matter"

I was never into that. I have an easier time than some in confronting people in a way they don't realize they're being confronted. But at the same time, I do it less and less. I've found it never really gets you anywhere, except perhaps to make the other person more defensive. I certainly didn't think it was ever going to help with my relationship with my parents.

Rather than responding in anger towards them, I responded by being depressed. It was my emotion of choice. In retrospect, I had a lot to be depressed about. But I didn't want to be a victim either. I didn't want the deficiencies in my childhood to define me. As I grew older, and started to consider how Jesus wanted me to live, forgiveness seemed the way to go. For me, forgiveness started when I was nineteen.

I was on my way home from college one fall Friday night sitting in the back of a Greyhound bus on Interstate 94 heading east into Milwaukee. I was thinking about my awful childhood and spending the upcoming weekend at home, wanting to be there, yet at the same time not wanting to. That's when it came to me, at the crest of the hill on I-94 near the west side of town, looking east to the skyline of Milwaukee. What little skyline we have was lit up and clearly visible. When that scene came into view, God slowly and gently impressed something on my heart, not in an audible whisper into my ear, but a whisper into my heart concerning my ambivalence about returning home.

You know, they did the best they could. Yes, you needed more and deserved more, like any kid. No doubt about it. But they did the best they could. So could you cut them a little slack? Do you think you could do this?

A sudden weight lifted from me that night on the crest of the hill overlooking the city. I think I could do this, I think I could cut them a little slack. For the first time, I started to think about their lives, and what it must be like for them, both in the present and the past. I thought of the unwise decisions they made and the consequences of those decisions. And from those thoughts seeped a measure of compassion from my heart, followed by forgiveness. It didn't come from gritting my teeth and doing something I felt obligated to do. It didn't come from trying harder. No, it was rather easy because the compassion and forgiveness really came from Jesus and what he was doing to soften me.

I thought of my dad and his father who died when he was quite young. Who was there to model for him what it meant to be a father? My dad was very much an extrovert and it must have been hard living with my introverted mother. He was a life-of-the-party kind of guy, which I think my mother enjoyed, but from a distance.

His mother, my grandmother, lived with us for a few years when I was very young, and I remember she and Mom argued often. There was a great deal of tension between the two of them. It must have been hard for my dad to deal with being caught in the middle between his wife and his mother.

He was loyal and faithful to my mom and never cheated on her. They were married forty-seven years when he died in 1997. While I wish he had been more involved in my life, he did teach me things. Like how to throw a curve ball and a change-up. I remember one particular time, he was teaching my brother and me these two pitches in our backyard. He threw an incredibly slow off-speed pitch to me that I whiffed at so terribly with my bat that he and my brother doubled over with gut-busting laughter.

"How do you do that? Show me how you do that!" I responded. He showed me all right, but I could never do it as well as he did. I did enjoy his laugh, though. Dad also taught us how to ice skate and how to do a figure-eight. He was a very good ice skater and would often take us skating on winter weekends. One routine he did, which I always marveled at, was his spread eagle. It's where you get some momentum going and end up skating in a big circle, facing outward with both feet pointed in the opposite direction, gliding on the outer edges of your ice skates.

"It's all about maneuvering your feet on the inner and outer edges of your skates," he would explain. I tried imitating all his moves, but the only things I could duplicate were a figure-eight and skating backwards. I wonder how he learned to skate so well. Who taught him?

The more years that pass, the more questions I would like to ask my parents. Questions only they could answer.

My dad also used ice skates to teach me about working hard to get something you want. By the time I was fourteen, my skates were too small for my growing feet. I asked for a new pair, but rather than just buying them for me, Dad told me I had to work for them. As one of five children, each one of us would take turns drying the dinner dishes each evening that our mother dutifully washed by hand. I hated this once-every-fifth-day-household chore. The challenge my dad laid before me was this, "If you dry the dishes every single night for one month, we'll buy you a new pair of ice skates."

My brother and three sisters were elated, encouraging me to accept the challenge. I so appreciated their concern for my character development.

I just dropped my shoulders, rolled my eyes, and groaned like teenage boys do. But I accepted the challenge, and got my pair of ice skates, which I have to this day because they still fit. This was my first experience at wanting something really important to me and having to work hard to get it. My dad taught me this essential value.

Of all the memories of my dad, however, the one that sticks out the most is the day Bozo died. I cringe now even using his name, but that is what we all affectionately called Mark, a neighbor boy who lived across the street. To refer to him now as Mark seems disrespectful. We all loved Bozo. Our neighborhood had lots of kids who hung around together, and we all got along well with each other. He was an integral part of our community, a community torn apart the evening Bozo was killed.

It was a few days after school started in September and my brother and I had just gone downstairs to do our homework in our basement bedroom—our boy cave. Suddenly, we heard unexpected footsteps coming down the stairs. It was our mother. Visibly shaken, she sat on one of our beds.

"I have some very bad news to tell you."

There was a long pause as she started to choke up, and then composed herself.

"Bozo was riding his bike home from a park late this afternoon and was hit by a car. And he died."

He died? Bozo is dead? How can that be? We just saw him yesterday. *How could he be dead?* I wondered. *That just can't be.*

Quietly sobbing, my mother went back upstairs. Shortly thereafter, my brother Joe and I followed upstairs. I remember all of us wandering around in disbelief, like disoriented ants, not knowing what to think and feeling quite shocked. With dusk setting in, I looked out a window and saw something I will never forget. There was Bozo's father, walking down the middle of the street of our quiet sleepy neighborhood, with my dad beside him, arm over his shoulder. My dad was no grief counselor. He had no training in this area, but he was a good neighbor and he cared for his friend. When I hear the expression "walking with someone through difficult times," I think of this image of my dad, who did this literally and figuratively for a neighbor whose son had just been killed.

I can't help but admire a man like that. For though he didn't treat me as well as he should have, he did the best he could. Relating to adults was easier for him; he was just unskilled in relating to his oldest son, who biologically was not his own. Yeah, I can have compassion for a dad like that, who had compassion for a grieving friend. I can forgive someone like him. Sure. I can do that. I should do that. I want to do that, so I will. I will forgive. And I did.

Then there's my mom. She did the best she could, too. I remember her always being uptight and nervous, and easily frustrated. Managing a household with five kids in a really small house must have been hard on her. There was always the sense we didn't have enough money as a family, so my mother tried to cut expenses as best she could. When I was a teenager, she encouraged me to drink coffee and less milk to save money. She made our clothes at times, and grew a vegetable garden in the backyard.

I don't remember my dad helping her much. Most husbands in the 1950s didn't either. Roles were more clearly segmented then than they are now. My mom wanted to get a part-time job to help with the finances, but Dad would not hear of it. Husbands in the fifties didn't hear a lot of things, and this was one of them.

One of the issues that got her uptight was my dad and his drinking habits. He would often stop for a few beers on his way home from work when his shifted ended at 11:00 p.m. Then on weekends, he would often hang out at a corner tavern near our house. Often he'd be late for dinner, which frustrated Mom to no end. It got to the point where if he was real late, she'd call the bar and ask to talk to him. In the male world of bar bonding, this was not good. Not good at all. I remember them arguing over it many times.

One summer afternoon during a severe attack of boredom, I begged my mother to play catch with me. Dad was at work, my brother wasn't around, and my sisters, well, they each threw a baseball like a girl. The only one left was Mom. She reluctantly stopped what she was doing, took off her apron (which was part of the 1950s mom uniform) and followed me to the backyard to play catch. We didn't do it for long, and like my sisters, she also threw like a girl. But it was enough for me. Enough to ease the boredom. And looking back on it many years later, enough to show me she was trying, and doing the best she could.

A number of years ago, I took my two sisters living in town out to lunch. My youngest sister lived in Florida, so it was just the three of us. I asked them what they remembered about our childhood, then I shared what it was like for me. They seemed a little surprised at what a bad stage of life it had been for me. But in hearing them describe their frame of reference, it seemed as each additional child came along, my parents grew wiser and more skilled in their parenting. I didn't benefit from it, but I was glad my brother and sisters did. It made it easier for me to give my parents the benefit of the doubt. It made it easier knowing they got better at parenting.

Janet and I then invited my brother Joe and his wife over for dinner and I asked him the same thing I asked my sisters, "What was childhood like for you?" Joe said it was a great time for him. He talked about Dad taking him to the corner bar to play pool. A wave of disappointment washed over me when he mentioned this, because I never was part of it. It very well may have happened when I left home for college, in which case it shows again my parents were doing a better parenting job with my siblings who came after me. They made progress, I thought. It made it easier to forgive them for how they parented me. It made it easier to find compassion for them in a hidden place in my heart.

Joe mentioned he thought Mom and Dad were usually much harder on me than on him and our sisters. When I was away at college, they told him and my three sisters what Mom told me when I was ten—that I was born illegitimate and Dad adopted me when I was eighteen months old. I was a bit surprised they knew. They had never brought it up with me before.

In thinking about my mom, I imagine the shame she must have felt as an unwed mother in 1949. She never told her parents or siblings about me until long after she married my dad a year and a half after I was born. Several years ago, I went to visit her sisters—my aunts—in northwestern Minnesota to learn more about my family history. They told me my mother mentioned me to them when I was a toddler, but they always suspected something was not quite right. So I filled them in on my story. Imagine not being able to talk to your parents or siblings about something like your own child? The more I thought about Mom and what life must have been like for her, the easier it was to have compassion for her. It reminded me of an axiom I've come to embrace:

If we knew more about each other, we'd sin against each other less.

A sinful response to someone you have compassion for doesn't exist together. Knowing more about someone and what a person has come through allows compassion and forgiveness to flow more freely. It's like untangling a crimp in a garden hose so water can flow again. I experienced this first hand with my mother shortly after she died in 2003.

Several days after her funeral, one of my sisters and I were cleaning out her apartment, where I found a notebook with the names and addresses of her friends. I called each of them to tell them of Mom's death. One in particular was a roommate she had when I was born, Kay Sommers. We called her Aunt Kay growing up. I was seventeen the last time I saw her in person. She had introduced my parents to each other and remained friends with them long after they married. Growing up, we would see her occasionally until she moved to California, where she lives today.

After expressing her condolences when I told her of Mom's passing, she began telling me more about my mother before she got pregnant with me. Kay was quite engaging and volunteered a great deal of information to the few questions I asked. She described where she and another roommate, Sally, lived with my mother in what is now a seedy part of Milwaukee. She told me that when I came on the scene, Mom was afraid to tell her family about me for fear they would disown her. The more Kay talked, the more questions came to mind, but it was getting late and she needed to end the call. Too many questions, too little time. I concluded the conversation by giving her a brief update of what was happening with my brother and sisters, and then I hung up. The March 2003 reconnection with Kay left me with a greater appreciation for my mom.

I wondered if I would ever talk to Kay Sommers again.

Nine years passed from the day of that conversation with Kay. Then on January 12, 2012, she called and left a voice mail message. Kay was updating her phone and address book and wanted to see if the phone number she had for me was still accurate.

"Call me some time if you're interested," she said.

I did. And I was. The very next day.

I had a question.

"Mom told me she worked two jobs for a time, but when she was working, who watched me? Did you or Sally babysit? Weren't the two of you working, too?"

Kay's answer to my question came as a jolt, the kind you get from plugging a defective lamp cord into an electrical outlet, where sparks fly everywhere. It so startled me, so stunned me, it was second only to the surprise of my mother telling me at age ten that I was adopted.

Chapter 14

Three Surprises

Of course it should not be too surprising to find out that your life story has included an event, something important, that you have known nothing about – your life story is in and of itself something that you know very little about.
—Philip Roth

I thought it was a simple question I asked Aunt Kay, "Who took care of me when my mother was working her telephone operator job by day, and her bowling alley-bar-maid job by night?" I expected a simple answer, thinking maybe Mom's roommates took turns babysitting. I assumed that for years, but I also knew Kay had a full-time career herself, so it was always a bit of a mystery to me.

"Who took care of you?" Kay asked. "Didn't your mother tell you? Sally and I both had full-time jobs. Your mother put you in a foster home for the first year and a half of your life until she married your dad."

What? How can this be? Not another surprise about my past. Not another secret my mother kept from me. Feeling a little angry at her for never telling me, I wondered why my mother kept it from me. There was a long silence on the phone while I processed the revelation, and I couldn't tell if Kay sensed my irritation or not.

Breaking the silence, Kay said, "There was a severe housing shortage after World War II in the late 1940s. If our landlord knew there was a single unmarried woman living in his building with a baby, he would have thrown us all out of our apartment. She had to keep your birth a secret. When she was getting far enough along in her pregnancy, she took a leave of absence from her job as a telephone operator. She told her employer there was an 'illness' in her family that required her care. If her boss knew the truth, she would have been fired. That's how it was in those days.

"Misericordia Hospital had a wing for unwed mothers and your mother moved in there while she was pregnant with you and worked at the hospital for her room and board."

I knew some part of the story from my mother, but had never heard any of the details Kay was sharing. I didn't know Mom moved into the hospital under an assumed name, and that she had to keep everything confidential to keep her job and apartment after I was born.

Kay continued, "The hospital was run by nuns and they assumed your mother would give you up for adoption when you were born. She didn't, of course. I visited her quite often while she lived there."

"What do you remember of the foster home I lived in?" I asked.

"It was a private home, very clean, where a young couple cared for you and one or two other babies. They were very nice. Your mother and I would visit you every Thursday until she married your dad."

By this point in our conversation, my initial reaction moved from anger to compassion for my mother. I thought of the energy it must have taken to maintain her secret. Secrets have a way of sapping our energy.

"What about my birth father, Jack Byrd? What do you remember about him?"

"I only met him once. They met at a dance."

There was a long pause.

"It's important you know your mother was not that kind of woman. She didn't hang around men and do that kind of thing. When she discovered she was pregnant with you, she wrote him a letter asking for help. He wrote back with just an awful letter, as I remember it, telling your mother he was married and to stop bothering him. Your mother was heartbroken.

"Abortion never entered your mother's mind. She wanted to keep you even though the nuns tried to persuade her to give you up for adoption."

So I spent my first year and a half in a foster home? Really?

Why hadn't I been told? This tapped into the theme I heard before—there are some things people aren't telling me. My mother didn't tell me until I was ten about Dad adopting me out of my illegitimacy. And now I learned I spent my earliest days under the care of strangers, and that my mom had to keep me a secret.

Maybe this is why I ask so many questions all the time. It drives Janet crazy sometimes.

I know there was never going to be a good time for my mother to tell me about the circumstances surrounding my birth. My hunch is she felt shame about putting me in foster care. I get that. But it's still troubling. So many times, I wish she was still around so I could ask her more questions, to find out more about what life was like for her. But she's gone now, and so is my dad. So my questions will have to remain unanswered.

After our phone call ended, I realized Kay had only been twenty-one years old when I was born, and there she was, helping my twenty-four-old-year-old mother with an illegitimate pregnancy on her hands. Kay didn't come out and say it, but I got the strong impression she had also helped my mother financially.

I need to call her again. Maybe even go to California to visit her for a few days, though she might find that odd. I don't know. I do know I will be calling her again.

Mother's Day was just a month away from when our conversation ended. I sent Kay flowers to mark the occasion. She has never been a mother, so I'm pretty sure she had never gotten Mother's Day flowers, but she was such an important part of my mom's life, I felt this would be a way to honor her and thank her for the care she showed to Mom, and to me, many years ago. In a card that came with the flowers, I told her how much I appreciated how she helped my mother through those difficult days—which in turn helped me, too.

Hearing Kay talk about her former roommate gave me a greater understanding of what life must have been like for my mother. There she was, a twenty-four-year-old farm girl living in the big city with no family around she could confide in or draw support from. More grace and compassion for her seeped out from my heart. She made many mistakes in her time, but she did the best she could. The best she knew how.

Several years after Dad retired, I got a phone call from Mom to tell me she was at the hospital with Dad. She called 911 when he fell out of his chair watching TV, and then rode with him in an ambulance to the hospital. He had suffered a stroke and would be staying in the hospital. She asked if I could come and pick her up, as there was nothing more she could do that night.

I drove down to the hospital to get her and take her back home, which became the first of many such trips with her. She still drove herself, but was quite nervous about this dramatic change in her life. So for those first few weeks, I often picked her up and we visited Dad together. On one such occasion, coming home after a hospital visit, we stopped for a red light at an intersection close to her home, the home where I spent almost all of my growing-up years.

As we came to a stop, she suddenly burst into tears and cried out, "I am so sorry for how I raised you. All the yelling and hitting. You didn't deserve any of that. I am so sorry. I am so sorry."

Here my dad, her husband, nearly died and was lying paralyzed in a hospital bed unable to speak and she's overcome with remorse about how she parented me over thirty years ago. The fact I forgave her many years earlier made it easier to respond to her out of compassion.

"That's okay, Mom. You did the best you could. I know that. You don't have to beat yourself up over this. I know you did the best you could."

Over the next several years, my mother wrote me two letters apologizing for how she treated me in my early years. They prompted me to write her the following note,

> *Dear Mom,*
>
> *I want you to know how grateful I am for all you've done for me. While I know it's probably not the easiest thing for you to talk about, I find as I learn more about my early past with you that I've come to appreciate you more and all the struggles you went through in raising me.*
>
> *I'm grateful you did not get an abortion when you were pregnant with me, and I'm grateful you did not give me up for adoption when I was born. I really appreciate how you worked two jobs to support me. I know it must have been hard on you.*
>
> *And I'm glad you named me John Michael - I really like my name. I'm glad you named me after your father's brother.*
>
> *I'm also grateful for Dad adopting me and helping to raise me, too. Thanks for being a good mother.*
>
> *Love,*
>
> *John Michael*

The last apology letter she wrote to me said in part,

> *"... I was hard on you lots of times for various things. I think now that I expected too much of you, even though you were still so young. I know I slapped you around a lot, and in retrospect, I'm sure I was lashing out at your father. For that I'M SORRY.*

I was always worried you would turn out to be like him. You proved me wrong, and for that, I'm proud of you. You proved to both Dad and me you had what it takes to be someone. You made it through four years of college on your own and I'm proud of you for that, although I never thought you would be a teacher. But you did. Then when you gave up teaching and started doing what you are doing now, I was a little apprehensive. But you did it. AND I'M PROUD OF YOU FOR THAT!!

Anyway, I know this letter doesn't make up for all the bad times, and the times I never said I love you, but I do love you and I'm darn proud of what you have made of your life.

Love,

Mom

You have to admire a woman who comes clean with what she did wrong and tries to make amends. I've re-read her letter several times over the years when I periodically purge my files. The most recent time, I was struck by her high degree of self-awareness. I was so glad I did not confront her with any of what she did. She figured that out on her own. Maybe God whispered into her heart, too, just like He did into mine when I was nineteen on the Greyhound bus driving up over the crest of I-94 heading into Milwaukee. I was so glad I forgave her many years before she apologized and wrote the two letters to me. I told her after each one that she didn't need to keep apologizing and to stop berating herself. I didn't need for her to say anything, or write anything, because it's what you do when you forgive.

It's a solo act with no backup singers.

It's *a cappella.*

No musical accompaniment needed.

Her apologies to me were more for her than they were for me. And that's great, it really is. What they did for me was confirm I wasn't crazy, that I hadn't made up memories of my dysfunctional childhood in my head. She confirmed reality for me. The reminder of what I forgave my parents for took the edge off the offense. There is something powerful and healing when others realize and acknowledge the harm they have done you. It was a wonderful gift my mother gave me. Totally unnecessary and totally unexpected.

So there you have it, two surprises. Finding out my early days were spent in a foster home, and then my mother breaking down in my car and apologizing for how she raised me. As if that weren't enough, just recently, I got a third surprise that was just as unexpected. It was something I thought would never happen. Something I thought was laid to rest years ago. Something I assumed I would never have to deal with again.

Rick, my former colleague and pastor, who had lied to me and threw me under the bus seven years ago, contacted me.

He asked if he could meet with me.

Chapter 15

Beyond Forgiveness

Forgiveness is the fragrance that the violet sheds
on the heel that has crushed it.
—Mark Twain

I was sitting at my desk, minding my own business, the day it came. I was at my computer, just starting to write the chapter on forgiveness for this book. Out of nowhere pops up a Facebook message from Rick.

> Hi John,
> Wondering if you would be willing to get together briefly, John. I am needing to ask for your forgiveness for the way I treated you several years back when we worked together at the church. To be in person, naming the ways I offended, is important to me. I apologize for the out-of-the-blue nature of this request, but the Holy Spirit is really convicting me to make some things right. If you don't want to meet, I understand. You can Facebook, call or e-mail me.
>
> In Christ,
> Rick

When I saw his message, I gulped and thought, *Oh, no, I don't want to do this. Life is going along really well for me. I don't want to complicate it. I don't want to go back and sift through all that smelly garbage again. I don't, I really don't. I've got too many other things to do. And why after seven years does he want to talk to me now? Why now, when I'm starting to write about forgiveness and reconciliation?*

I'd much rather write about it than do it.

In reading Rick's message, I wonder if he remembered the last conversation Janet and I had with him seven years ago in his office. I told him at the time, I forgave him, along with what I needed from him in order for us to reconcile. I said I would need him to admit his sin, acknowledge the harm he caused me, show remorse for it, and commit to work at never repeating the offense again. Was Rick wanting to reconcile now? I didn't get any of what I asked for when we talked seven years ago, but this had nothing to do with my forgiving him. His actions, or lack of them, did not negate what was incumbent on me: to forgive him.

Lack of forgiveness and its debilitating effects are much easier to see in someone else than in ourselves. To forgive another for the harm he or she has caused us is difficult, but if we don't forgive, we end up harming ourselves, often without realizing how we're self-destructing. It occurred to me one day that forgiveness is a lot like losing weight.

Both require us to say "No" to something we want. In relating to others, it's saying "No" to our right to make someone pay for an injustice we've suffered at their hands. With losing weight, it's saying "No" to the pleasure food brings, pleasure we're entitled to from time to time. Both losing weight and forgiveness require us to relinquish our rights. Forgiving someone who hurt us, and working to lose weight, require personal sacrifice. Both take time. Done well, both of them bring freedom and energy to our lives. Often, however, just when we think we've mastered both, we fall backwards. So we start all over again.

The cost of withholding forgiveness, or failing to lose unwanted weight, is very high. Both have a perceived benefit that is alluring, but false. To hang on to our rights for justice has the enticing benefit of letting us live as victims, for it requires nothing of us. It's all about the other guy and what he's done. It's something from the past we can re-live over and over again, like endless late night re-runs of *Seinfeld* and *M*A*S*H*. It's like going to the refrigerator and eating cold left-overs day after day, hoping each time they will taste just as good as they did when served hot out of the oven several days before. But with each bite, we just swallow more disappointment.

Withholding forgiveness is never being fully present in the here and now because the pain of the back then and there consumes us. Drains us. Saps us of our energy. To cling to our right to make someone pay for what he or she has done to us is to live with the illusion that somehow justice will prevail, the guilty will be discovered, and we will be exonerated.

Sadly, even when we do let someone off the hook, it often doesn't change how the person who harmed us relates to us. But that's not the point. Not to be confused with reconciliation, which takes two to make happen, forgiveness is always something we can extend on our own. It doesn't matter how the other person responds.

How, then, do we relinquish our right to justice? This takes supernatural power that only comes from Jesus. It's calling upon God to give us what we need to let go, to relinquish our rights, to trust Him to render justice in His due time.

I saw an example of this some time ago when a missionary talked to Janet and me about the harm done to her and her family by her colleagues. It had been several years since the offense occurred, and yet she thought about it almost daily. She knew she had to forgive, and she wanted to. But it was hard. After talking to her about the situation for several months, there came a breakthrough when she realized, "You know, this is all taking way too much of my time and energy. What a waste it's been to keep thinking about this. There's stuff I want to do and this is getting in the way. What a waste!"

Like losing weight, forgiving someone starts with a choice. We can chose to continue carrying around unwanted pounds because it feels better than saying "No" to the pleasure food brings. Or we can relinquish our right to feel good now, knowing we'll feel even better in the future. It works like this in relationships, too. Half the battle in forgiving is wanting to.

In weight loss circles, you often hear the expression, *Nothing tastes as good as thin feels.* In forgiving others, a similar aphorism applies: *Forgiveness granted satisfies more than justice received.*

Forgiveness Doesn't Mean You Forget

One thing that makes forgiveness hard for people is equating forgiveness with reconciliation. If I forgive Uncle Charlie for sexually abusing me when I was nine years old, do I have to give him a big hug when he visits for Thanksgiving?

No. You don't even have to invite Uncle Charlie for Thanksgiving.

If I forgive Uncle Charlie, does that mean I need to forget about what he did? Just pretend it never happened? No. That would not be wise. A better question is, "Should I trust Uncle Charlie?"

While forgiveness is about relinquishing your right to make others pay for how they harmed you, reconciliation is different. You can forgive without reconciliation, but you can't reconcile without forgiveness. Our forgiving another depends solely on us, regardless of how the other party responds or doesn't respond. But reconciliation depends on the response of both parties. It depends on my forgiving the other person, the other party owning up to what happened, and a commitment to not letting history repeat itself.

Once that happens, there's still a challenge for the one forgiven. It's dealing with "He said he forgave me. Now why can't we just move on and get along? What's wrong with him?"

What's wrong is that trust has been broken.

I can forgive people, yet not trust them. At least not trust until they demonstrate trustworthy behavior. This makes it harder for the person sinned against than the sinner. It's tough to trust someone after we've been betrayed. It really is. We have the tendency to be super-vigilant and view every action of others through the filter of what they did to us in the past. If those who have offended can't appreciate this, it makes you wonder if they truly understand the damage they caused.

The challenge goes back to forgiveness. If I've really forgiven others, it means I've given up my right to have them pay for their wrongdoing. I'm letting go. But if I refuse to look for ways to trust people who have hurt me, if I don't give others a chance to prove themselves again, if I suspect every action, then it brings into question whether I truly have forgiven.

We need to take a risk and give others a chance to earn back our trust. When we take that risk, it's quite possible we'll be hurt again. Be cautious. Be alert, but take the risk nevertheless.

* * * * *

After the meeting I had in Rick's office seven years ago, and his stone-cold response to what I needed from him to reconcile, I thought it was the last I was ever going to see of him. My forgiveness of him was a done deal, though. In the bag. Reconciliation? It seemed highly unlikely then. But now he contacts me after seven years. I'm going to have to put up or shut up.

In his Facebook message, Rick gave me several ways to get back to him about meeting, but I wasn't ready to talk yet. I needed time to process this unexpected disruption to my life. The feeling was like thoroughly weeding a flower bed, only to discover weeds I thought I uprooted and killed had returned.

Reconciliation with my parents was a lot different. I forgave them, just as I forgave Rick. But I didn't feel the need to tell them how awful they had parented me. There wasn't one event that occurred, like there was with Rick, to drive us apart. They were imperfect people, doing the best they could with the limitations they had. Reconciliation with them was more about me extending grace and accepting their weaknesses and imperfections. They just didn't know any better.

Rick did.

Reconciliation with him was going to be very different. He had not done the best he could. He was capable of much more.

We used e-mails and Facebook to communicate with each other to set a time and place to meet. Our meeting date was almost two weeks from his first Facebook communication with me. I needed time to consider how I was going to respond. I needed to remind myself what had originally happened between the two of us. I needed time to think how he might possibly respond, and then how in turn I would react.

Is he really sincere about wanting my forgiveness, or was this something simply to relieve his guilt? Did he have any clue at all as to the damage he caused me? Did he know what he needed forgiveness for? I wasn't going to find out until we met face to face. Maybe I should be prepared to walk out of the meeting if it doesn't go well—sit close to the door and all that. Maybe I should remain guarded and say as little as possible. I was beginning to feel like I was going into a chess match. *This is nuts,* I thought.

I didn't know what would happen, but I did know the truth about who I am. I knew I was not the person he said I was back then. I wasn't going to give him power to define me. The only thing that mattered was what God thought of me. If there was something I needed to change about who I was, then it was up to God to point that out to me. We all play to an audience of one. God's opinion of us is the only one that matters.

Rick and I by then had both moved on to other churches. He asked me where I would like to meet and I said I could come down to his new church where he was a pastor. He met me at the door at the appointed time, then ushered me into a meeting room where we sat and exchanged pleasantries for a few minutes. I let him take the lead.

After a deep sigh, he began to speak.

"John, thank you for meeting with me. I felt it important to meet with you face to face to ask your forgiveness for the way I treated you several years ago back when we were both at the other church working together.

"I was arrogant in how I treated you, which you didn't deserve, and I want to apologize for that. I was wrong and I'm so sorry for this. If it helps you any, I want you to know I don't view you through the lens of what I accused you of before. I know you to be a godly, caring man and I have no question at all about your integrity. I want you to know that."

I just listened, trying to hold back the tears from those old wounds. It hurt to revisit the pain I had worked through and put to rest.

"Thank you," I said. "You may have forgotten this, but when we last talked, I told you I did forgive you. I've worked through how you viewed me, but hearing you now does help. Looking back, what would you have done differently?" I asked.

"I got caught up in gossip that was swirling around then, and I wish I would have checked into things more instead of making assumptions," Rick replied. "I learned that I develop a theory about a person and then filter everything through that theory. But this is very wrong."

"Is there anything you think I should have done differently?" I asked.

"No. Nothing at all," he responded.

Any doubts I had about Rick and his sincerity and motives began to evaporate like a brief, unexpected rain shower off a sizzling hot concrete sidewalk. His eyes, too, began to leak like mine. It was painful for him as well.

"I mean," he continued, "to refer you on to another pastor, and then to make you go for counseling—how demeaning and shaming it was of me."

I had forgotten about that part. I forgot when Mike, the first counselor Rick sent me to, said he thought my problem was something I needed to work out with Rick, how Rick said he couldn't deal with me, and that he was referring me to Kevin, the pastor over Rick. It had been demeaning and shaming. Kevin, Rick's boss, was of no help at all; in fact, he made things worse. He made things worse because he didn't do anything. At the end of my time of counseling with Don, I asked Kevin to contact Don so I could be restored to ministry in the church. Don saw nothing in me that disqualified me, and I wanted Kevin to know this. He never contacted Don, in spite of my two requests to do so. I tried to set that whole dynamic aside to concentrate on what Rick had to say.

"This has been a terrible couple of years for me at this new church," Rick continued. "I knew there were problems when I came here, but I thought with all my experience, I could have a positive impact. But it's been months and months of being attacked and criticized for things that aren't true. People are making assumptions about me that are false, and as I've been dealing with this, God spoke to me by saying, 'You know, Rick, you did the same thing to John years ago that people are now doing to you.' So that's how the Holy Spirit prompted me to try to make things right with you. I know how it feels, and I'm so sorry for what I did to you."

"I am sorry you have to deal with this," I said, my heart hurting with his.

"Well, thank you, I appreciate you saying that. You know, when I contacted you to get together, I thought 'No way is he going to want to meet after the damage I did to him.' I was so relieved when you said you were willing to get together.

"I have tried reaching out to seven other people to ask for their forgiveness for how I've treated them," Rick continued, "but not one of them has been willing to get together with me as you have. They all tell me they're too hurt, too wounded. So the fact you have met with me feels like a big weight has been lifted off my shoulders. Thank you."

As we neared the end of our conversation, Rick said, "I don't know what the future holds, but I would hope maybe there might be something we can join forces on together."

"I'd like that very much," I said.

Our conversation ended with both of us getting up from our chairs and Rick giving me a hug. I hugged right back. As great as forgiveness is, reconciliation is even better. Rick's wanting to make things right with me helped make sense of the past, and my response lifted a burden from him. We cared well for each other. It was a really good day.

I returned home and told Janet what happened. I was emotionally exhausted. Our meeting turned out better than I had ever imagined. It brought to mind all the things I liked about Rick before we split. It reminded me of what a quality person he is. To initiate our meeting like he did, to admit where he was wrong, and to take ownership of his failure took humility and courage. How can you not be drawn to someone like that? The way he spoke to me and the tone of his comments revealed genuine remorse.

Like Rick, I don't know what the future will bring for our relationship. All I know now, today, is we're reconciled. How pleased God must feel, because two of His children, whom He loves beyond measure, are at peace with one another.

Chapter 16

Lifetime Achievement Awards
for Everyone

We value virtue but do not discuss it. The honest bookkeeper,
the faithful wife, the earnest scholar get little of our attention
compared to the embezzler, the tramp, the cheat.
—John Steinbeck, *Travels with Charley*

I love the story of Rick's and my reconciling because it's an example of hearing from God to work at repairing a damaged relationship. It's about being obedient to God in taking ownership of the pain we've caused, to set aside our pride, and to seek forgiveness. These are tools to repair what we broke. Much of caring for others is like this, fixing relationships. Solving a problem. Restoring what used to be. All good and necessary efforts. But there's more to caring for others than fixing relational problems.

Another way we can care for each other is to think of ways we can encourage one another, to build each other up to be the best we can be. We don't need a problem to solve or an issue to fix to show genuine care. If the only way we care for each other is by helping to solve a problem, people become more a project than part of a relationship. Instead, we care well when we honor each other. Let me tell you a story about this.

One of the biggest adjustments Janet and I had to make in our marriage is how we do birthdays. I came from a family of seven where birthdays were no big deal. A card, a gift from my parents, and a cake from Mom were about it. It was over and done within about ten minutes. It was the same way for everyone in our family. Janet, however, came from a family where birthdays rivaled Christmas and the Second Coming in importance. There was not only the actual birthday itself, there was also birthday week. In the early years of our marriage, we compromised on this important tradition: we did birthdays the way she did.

But I must say, I do enjoy the hoopla we've created around them. I've done all manner of birthday surprises for Janet, like taking her places without telling her where we are going, and inviting friends over to surprise her. My favorite surprise was the time I suggested we drive with our young kids to the end of the city bus line, and then hop on the bus and ride to a pizza place we used to frequent in high school. In those days, we took the city bus everywhere, as neither of us drove. I persuaded Janet to take one more bus ride as we did as teenagers, for nostalgia's sake. They say now that nostalgia isn't what it used to be. I wore my high school letter jacket for the occasion, something I usually only wore when changing the oil in our car.

"Janet, I know it's twenty degrees out and windy, but that's what it was like for us back in high school. Our kids need to experience this. If not for me, then do it for the children. Do it for the children, Janet."

She wasn't too happy about the adventure, especially since we got on the bus at the end of the line where the driver takes a break before he heads back in the direction he came. It was a dark, cold night when we boarded the bus. We found one lone, suspicious passenger sitting in the very last seat in the rear, which only added to Janet's displeasure. Soon after we pulled away from the layover stop, however, Janet's mood began to change. At each stop along the way to the pizza place, a different set of friends got on the bus to join us, each dressed as they did when they were in high school.

I had sent our friends a map and bus schedule, and assigned each one a particular stop along the way where they were to board the bus.

Each subsequent stop evoked hilarious laughter as we picked up additional friends dressed as they had when teenagers.

The creepy passenger who was on the bus when we got on turned out to be a photographer for the *Milwaukee Journal*, our local newspaper. In preparing for the evening, I talked to someone in the feature department of the newspaper, suggesting perhaps their readers would be interested in reading about this unusual birthday celebration. When the bus reached our final destination, the photographer took a photo of me carrying Janet off the bus, which was printed the next day with a brief caption (misspelling my name) explaining the event.

Another part of the surprise was telling our guests ahead of time I would pay for pizza for everyone, as long as each person wrote a one-page essay, entitled *What January Twenty-Ninth Means to Me.* January twenty-ninth is Janet's, and Oprah's, birthday. The essays were belly-laugh funny.

In the years that followed, we added more to the birthday celebration. We started birthday eve, birthday week, and now birthday month. Then most recently, I came up with the Birthday Tree. This developed because of an after-Christmas sale where Janet bought a small, three-foot-high, artificial Christmas tree for the following year. I found a pedestal to put the tree on, and left it in the corner of our living room, waiting to be stored with the other Christmas decorations. By this time, it was early January, just a few weeks before Janet's birthday. So we left the tree on its pedestal in the corner, where family members later placed their birthday gifts for Janet. Our grandkids loved it. It's our new birthday tradition. The birthday tree.

So what's the big deal about birthdays?

The big deal is that it is about honoring someone.

It's about making someone the center of attention, at least for a few moments in the year. It's to show appreciation for others for no other reason other than they were born. It's to recognize someone not for any accomplishment, not for any achievement, not for any special gifts or talents he or she has. No, it's to honor someone for the simple fact of coming into the world and being a part of our lives.

Don't we all deserve this?

All of us are miracles, we really are. We need to celebrate that. The miracle of our birth is one thing that joins us all. I'm working on a theory that you can never honor others too much on their birthday, and that we could all do each other a big favor by looking for ways to honor one another, and one way is to overdo it when it comes to celebrating the day people were born.

For our grandkids, we stick our collection of small American flags in the ground up and down the driveway on their birthday. Grandsons George and Grant have birthdays in February, so the flags go in snow banks where we live.

A few years ago, we took our friend Rita out for pizza on her birthday in August. Every so often after that, we'll take her out again to celebrate her birthday, even if it's March or November. We do the same with our friend, Karla. You can never celebrate one's birthday too often. Limiting it to just one day a year doesn't do it justice.

I feel sorry for people who come from traditions where birthdays don't mean much. The emptiness of this can be soothed by choosing to honor others and taking vicarious pleasure in doing so. It works for me, that's for sure. The emptiness of what I feel because of whatever is missing in my own life is often filled by extending myself to others in ways that help fills the emptiness in their lives. You wouldn't think this would work, but it does.

One night while Janet was watching television, I was busy doing something else. To take a break from my something else, I wandered in to see what she was viewing. It was one of those interminable Hollywood shows in which they bestow a lifetime achievement award on one of its own. No other industry I know congratulates and applauds itself more than Hollywood.

"I think everyone should get a lifetime achievement award," I flippantly commented as I passed through the room.

Many months later, Janet arranged a get-together with our two adult children to celebrate my birthday. As a gift, they presented me with my own Lifetime Achievement Award. It is a 13 x 16-inch framed award, matted with beveled edges by my daughter and daughter-in-law, both of whom are talented graphic designers. The award reads:

On this day in history, February 27, 1999
John Michael Certalic
is hereby awarded the
Lifetime Achievement Award
for attaining the following accomplishments:

A list of thirty "accomplishments" followed, all simple things that were part of my persona, mostly inside family jokes. The first accomplishment on the list:

Outstanding Effort in Obtaining Ice Skates—1963

In Chapter 13 on forgiveness, I wrote how I earned the skates. I used to milk this story for all it was worth in raising our kids. It was my *we-had-to-walk-fifteen-miles-to-school-in-our-bare-feet-in-the-dead-of-winter* story most parents have up their sleeve. My ice skates story got old after the second time I told it, and the kids would just roll their eyes when they heard it yet again. Which is why I told it.

The other items on the list were about being the best in something, except for one: *Most organized home office, Honorable Mention*. I'm almost certain this was my son-in-law Tim's idea. There is nothing remotely resembling an organized home office in our house. And everyone in our family knows it, and have been trying to get me to change for years. I howled with laughter when I read it.

Nothing on my list of accomplishments would make the nightly news, or even the free community newspaper you find at grocery stores. But the fact there are people on this planet who know me well, and love me anyway, despite all my idiosyncrasies, makes this "award" priceless in my book. Everyone should be honored with his or her own lifetime achievement award.

We care for people when we honor them, as Janet and our kids did with me. We honor others when we're with them for the important milestones of life, like birthdays, and their child's wedding and their parent's funeral.

There's another way we can honor someone that takes less creativity and less money than a Lifetime Achievement Award. But it's costly and requires more of us, which is why there's so little of it going around these days. It's *listening* to someone. I mean really listening. We honor others when we truly listen to them. We honor others when we want to know what's on their mind and heart. We honor others when we work to understand what it's like to be them.

What a great gift it is to sit and listen to another. And while it's a sacrifice at times to listen, it is also a great privilege to have people share their hearts with us. It's quite an honor, actually. Plus for me, listening to the heart of another person pulls me out of the depressing hole I find myself in at times.

We honor another person when we set aside our needs for the moment so we can be fully present with that person. It's like we have a large box filled with all our needs and concerns. In it, we put decisions we have to make, what we need to pick up from the grocery store, worries about how the kids are doing in school, our loneliness, money problems, our exhaustion, and our to-do list. Stuff like that. We then put a lid on the box with all these needs, and put the box on the top shelf in our closet and close the door. We know our needs and problems will be safe there in the box, and we can come back to them after we are finished listening to someone. They will be waiting for us when we return. They won't go away, or be damaged. We then close the closet door so we can be fully present to focus our attention on another human being.

Listening is all about the other person, and nothing about us.

That's what listening looks like when it's done well. When we don't listen well, we have our box of needs right beside us with the cover off. We'll look at the other person, but every so often, glance down with our heart at our box of needs and concerns. Our eyes are looking straight ahead, and our heads are gently nodding, but our hearts are rummaging around in our open box. It's like texting while driving.

Looking like we're listening is much easier than listening itself. All the eye contact, nodding, "ah huh's," and other listening noises in the world can't make up for a heart that is distracted and thinking about oneself.

Maybe it's just me, but one interesting listening noise I notice common to missionaries comes out when they want to communicate they understand what the other person is saying. While another person is talking they'll interject, "Yeah-yeah-yeah." It's a reflex action that comes across to me as "I hear you, I know what you're talking about, I understand, so you really don't need to say anymore. In fact, I would really prefer we move on to the next thing because my attention span has reached its limit." Yeah-yeah-yeah just shuts me down. Silence would be a much better.

Silence, sweet silence, is a most underused listening skill. But for many of us, silence makes us uncomfortable. There's something within us that feels the need to fill silence with our words. Yet some of us need silence like we need water. A pastor friend of mine told me of a road trip he once took with his wife of many years, where they had frequent periods of silence in the car. At one point, he turned to her, sitting in the passenger seat, and said, "Carol, being with you is like being alone."

Whoa. What did that mean?

My friend went on to explain. "When I told Carol that being with her is like being alone, she smiled from ear to ear, for she knew exactly what I meant. We're both introverts at heart and so she knew I need to be alone to recharge, and that being with her re-charges me. We had reached a closeness in our marriage where I could say that."

It was one of the tenderest things I've heard in a long time.

For the rest of us, though, why is silence in our relationships such an awkward experience? I have a theory that silence makes us uncomfortable because we build so little of it into our lives. It startles us at times because of its unfamiliarity. It's like meeting someone at the mall you went to high school with who clearly remembers you, but you have no clue as to who they are. We fill those awkward moments with words to make the silence go away.

"Let silence do the heavy lifting," as Susan Scott says in her book, *Fierce Conversations*. Silence in conversations exposes our insecurities. I know it does for me. I wonder if people feel as awkward as I do at the moment, and what can I say to ease the awkwardness. Because isn't this my job, after all, to make sure others don't feel awkward?

Discomfort with silence in a relationship is all about what's going on inside of me. It's not a void we need to fill, for silence may be the very thing the other person needs to process what's being discussed. What seems like ten minutes of silence to us, may very well feel like a nano second to the other person when he or she is thinking hard about our conversation. If they really do feel uncomfortable and awkward, let them end the silence.

One healthy way we can end silence, and honor someone at the same time, is to ask questions. Questions with the right motive. The wrong reasons to ask questions of another start with wanting to control the conversation and relationship. It's to lead people down a path we want to go, and not necessarily where they want to go. Doing so doesn't honor other people, because it's all about us and little about them.

You see this when someone makes a statement, but disguises it as a question. "Aren't you going to take out the trash tonight?" really means, "Please take out the trash." It's more honest, and less manipulative to make a statement, than to hide the request in the form of a question.

Another impure motive for asking a question is to hide. I do this all the time. People have told me I'm a good listener, partly because I ask questions of others. But there are times I do this out of a sense of self-protection. When I don't want to talk, or if I feel someone is getting too close to something sensitive that is troubling me, I'll find a way to shift the spotlight off of me to shine on the other person. While on the surface it looks good, underneath it's often a way I cover my discomfort.

I've had too many experiences where I've shared something eating away at my heart, and people's eyes glaze over. They change the subject, or respond by talking about themselves or their Aunt Agnes who has the same problem I have. I often don't want to talk about the deep things going on inside of me because when I have in the past, it hurts when people don't listen well. So if I keep my distance, you won't have an opportunity to ignore me. You won't hear what's troubling me, and you won't confirm my deep-down fear that you really don't care. This, of course, does nothing to ease my loneliness, but at least it doesn't make it worse. And at times, that's the best I can hope for.

It's not just me, though. I see it all the time, as I did in a Bible study group several years ago. One night, a woman in the group talked about the pain of infertility. She and her husband wanted a second child, but it just wasn't happening. It bothered her greatly. But there was no acknowledgement of how troubling this was to her by anyone in the group, myself included. A few of us nodded, then someone changed the subject by bringing up something that was bothering him. I wish now I would have said something to her, something to at least acknowledge how hard the challenge must be for her and her husband. My silence and poor listening caused her the same pain I've experienced from others.

Just recently, Janet and I sat across a table from a missionary we hadn't seen in about four years. I told her how much I enjoyed reading her e-mail updates of what she and her husband were doing overseas. We both knew, because of circumstances out of our control, we only had about ten minutes to talk. Ten minutes to catch up on four years.

"So how are you and Paul doing?" I asked.

"We're fine. It's been a hard season for us, but we're fine. But I really want to hear about you and what you're up to."

"Oh, we're fine, too. We're doing okay," I responded. "How are your kids doing? We just saw them the other day."

"They're okay, too. But seriously, we only have a few minutes together. I really do want to know how the two of *YOU* are doing."

It was a like a cool refreshing splash of water to my face on a hot summer afternoon. People rarely press me like she did. She was truly interested. And I could tell she wasn't trying to hide or protect herself, as I sometimes do. She really did care. My "I'm feeling fine" was not going to do it for her. It reminded me of what I heard awhile back about how "fine" is an acronym for Feelings Inside Not Expressed. F.I.N.E.

I didn't know how to respond to her genuine inquiry into my life. I really didn't. I've not had much practice in answering such a question in the way she asked it. I don't remember what I said, but I felt free to share. I felt I could trust her. My guard dropped. And I felt honored.

We honor others when we inquire into their lives out of genuine interest in them and the journey they are on. Inquiry with no strings attached. Asking other people about their lives gets attention off ourselves and shifts it to the other person. It's a way of connecting with someone.

So when I give talks on becoming a better listener, I routinely talk about asking questions. I found many people would like to ask questions, but they just don't know what to ask. *No problem,* I thought. I'll just give people a list of questions they can use with just about anyone. But as I developed this list, it became obvious to me I was making a simple matter more complicated than it really was. *Who's going to remember my list of thirty-five questions, as brilliant as they are*? No, there's got to be an easier way. I threw away my list of questions and reduced them to just two questions. Two questions to remember that will serve us well when we want to inquire into the life of another in ways that honor the person. Just two simple questions.

The first is a question we ask ourselves, *What must it be like to be that person?* When we ask this question of ourselves, other questions will naturally flow. They'll naturally flow if we've taken all our needs and concerns and put them in a box, closed it with a lid, and put it on the top shelf of our closet, and closed the door on them.

For example, take the woman in our Bible study troubled by infertility. Even as a man, I can ask myself, *What must it be like to be her?* Out of this question other questions will arise like:

How are you and your husband dealing with this?
What's the worst part of it for you?
How are friends and relatives responding to you?
In dealing with this issue, is there anything that makes the pain of it more manageable for you?
Where is God in all of this for you? (This question, by the way, is a great question to ask most people going through difficulties.)

Unfortunately, in situations like the woman in our Bible study, we'll instead ask questions like, *Have you tried_____?* Or worse yet, *Why not adopt a child?* Both questions are attempts to make the problem go away, to "fix" things.

Our urge to fix is one we need to overcome if we are going to honor people. Advice and tips are not helpful when people are weeping over a deep-felt desire of their heart. Often our rush to fix another's problem stems from our self-centered discomfort with someone else's pain. We want their pain to go away so our discomfort with what they're going through will leave us too.

The second question we can always ask is pretty simple. It's a follow-up question. When someone answers our question, or makes a statement, ask a follow-up question. While it's a simple thing to remember, it can be hard to do. If we view our listening as waiting to talk, we're not going to want to ask a follow-up question because that will only delay the time when I'll be able to speak. Asking a follow-up question is hard when we're pre-occupied with our own needs and issues of life.

But asking a follow-up question is easy when we make the decision to be fully present with the person we're listening to. To be fully present is to keep a lid on the box of all the decisions, concerns, and things we have to do. When we're done listening, there will be plenty of time to go back and ruminate over all that is concerning to us. Being fully present with another makes honoring someone by listening to them a lot easier.

What do you mean by that is a great follow-up question. So is *can you give me an example of that.* And my all-time favorite is one a grandson of ours asks all the time, w*hy*.

I was in a group with pastors on one occasion when one of them made the comment, "I'd rather do a hundred funerals than one wedding." No one responded to what I thought was an intriguing comment, so I butted in and asked *why*. What followed was an interesting and lengthy response that engaged everyone in the group. All because of one simple follow-up question, w*hy*.

Life-giving conversations are those marked with talking in great depth about a few things. Life-draining encounters are filled with talking a little about many, many things. The next time you're in a conversation with someone, or listening to one, notice how many times the topic of conversation changes. The more it changes, the less listening is going on. Listening well to another is a great way to honor someone.

* * * * *

Someone else who deserves honor is God, more than anyone. He deserves a Lifetime Achievement Award. We can honor God in many ways. We honor Him when we obey Him, and when we care deeply about what He cares about. We honor Him when we relate well with Him.

I once took a test, the kind you find in *Ladies Home Journal,* that was supposed to reveal my preferred way of relating to God. I flunked the test. I remember flunking the test because I really wanted to connect with God through music, just like the rest of the people in our church who sing so well on Sunday morning. But I didn't. I don't even remember how I actually did connect with God, at least from the test results. All I can remember is that it wasn't through music, even though at times, the songs we sing in church will deeply move me and water my eyes. Maybe it goes back to my accordion days as a kid, but I envy people who can sing or play musical instruments. The best I can do is play the radio.

My one great fantasy is to be invited to be part of a flash mob singing *O, Holy Night* or Handel's *Hallelujah Chorus* in a really large multi-story shopping mall. Just like you see in those YouTube videos that show up each December. Even if I crashed one of these flash mobs and started singing, two notes into it, someone's bound to whisper in my ear, "Say, pal, I see Pottery Barn is having a special sale at the other end of the mall. I think you could find something there your wife would like. But the sale ends in ten minutes, so if I were you, I'd hurry on over there right now."

So if I have no musical ability whatsoever and cannot connect with God on that level, what's left? I was discouraged about my deficiency for many years until I came across a passage in the Bible that set me free. It's the Apostle Paul's letter to the Romans, chapter twelve.

In the first few verses, Paul tells us to offer our bodies as living sacrifices. By doing so, we're worshipping God. Okay, I get that. But how does this work? Paul goes on to say we shouldn't think more highly of ourselves than we should, but rather, think about ourselves objectively based on the faith God has given us. So far so good.

He then transitions from how we are to look at ourselves to how we are to view others. We're to view others as important parts of the same group we belong to, the body of Christ, even though we are all so very different. We all need each other.

To view people in this way is a sacrifice for me, because I would much prefer that everyone was like me. Same interests, same intelligence, same values. But viewing people as Paul describes is not only a sacrifice, it's also an act of worship. For I honor God when I place a high value on what He highly values—other people He created.

The rest of Romans 12 explains how, starting with getting out of the way and letting people be who God created them to be. Paul describes specific acts of behavior that are often sacrificial, and almost always worshipful:

Love with sincerity.
Hate evil.
Cling to what is good.
Devote yourself to one another based on love for them.

Honor others above ourselves.
Be zealous in serving the Lord.
Share with people.
Practice hospitality.
Bless those who persecute you.
Rejoice with those who rejoice.
Mourn with those who mourn.
Live in harmony with each other and don't be proud or conceited.
Don't repay evil with evil.
Do what's right.
Live at peace with everyone, as far as it depends on you.
Feed your enemies.
Overcome evil with good.

So relating well with people—loving them and honoring them—is a spiritual act of worship. It's hard, and it is a sacrifice, but I think I can do it. I can honor God without words. I can worship God without a song. What a relief! I'm feeling better already. With God's help, maybe someday I can earn another Lifetime Achievement Award for honoring others, which honors and worships God at the same time.

Chapter 17

Wheelchairs and Pogo Sticks

Our very lives are fashioned by choice.
First we make choices. Then our choices make us.
—Anne Frank

S everal years ago, Janet and I were asked to help a pastor friend
start a new church about twenty-five miles from our home. We
agreed to help him for six months, which among other things,
meant driving to his home twice a month for leadership meetings. I
always enjoyed these meetings because we worked with great people
whose company we thoroughly enjoyed. Those were good days, though
tarnished a bit by something that happened on our way to every
meeting.

Each time we met, I couldn't help but share what I saw on the way
in. It often delayed the start of the meeting because of my need to vent
and process my observation. What others found only mildly interesting
about my observation drove me to distraction.

On the way to these leadership meetings, Janet and I drove past a
small mom-and-pop retail furniture store. The sign along the highway
was half as big as the store itself, but that wasn't what bothered me. It
was the name of the store itself.

Just Oak and More.

Excuse me. *Just Oak AND More?*

"Just Oak," I get. "Oak and More." Sure, why not? Makes sense.

But "Just Oak and More?"

Come on, people. You can't have it both ways. If it's going to be "just" anything, it has to be just that. One thing, and nothing more. Even if the one thing is very broad, say *Just Books*. If you have a *Just Books* store, you'd better be just selling books, and not related paraphernalia. It could be all kinds of books—cookbooks, automobile manuals, fiction books, children's books, investment books, art books, decorating books. As long as it's a book. But please, in a *Just Books* store, no magazines, no bookmarks, no reading lights, no calendars or greeting cards. Nothing but books, get it? Let's show a little respect for the word "just."

A family friend is managing editor of *Just Between Us*. The name says a lot. *Us* they clearly define as women in ministry. So we know who the magazine is for and whom it's not for. It's not for truckers, vegetable growers, stamp collectors, or professional wrestling fans. It's *just* for women in ministry. I can live with that.

But if you can't live with "just," that's fine, too. I understand. I don't like feeling restricted either. Just be who you say you are. *Books and More* would be also fine with me. Sell tires, funeral plots, towels, yogurt, fishing poles, or jewelry—and even books. They're all entirely respectful of the word "more."

I don't even have a problem with "Christian Bookstore." In the typical Christian bookstore, usually one-third of the floor space actually contains books. The rest is taken up with what one retailer called "Jesus junk." The pictures, figurines, cards, coffee mugs, calendars—all the stuff with higher profit margins than books that allow the store to stay in business. I have no problem with that at all.

Just Oak and More, however, defies logic, marketing principles, and the English language.

Yet a lot of us live *Just Oak and More* lives.

We want it all. When it comes to all the attractive options of life open to us, we don't want to exclude any of them. Because if we do, we're afraid we'll miss out on something. We want the *Just* at the same time we want the *More*.

We want things that are mutually exclusive. One of the most mutually exclusive things we encounter is the mutually exclusive nature of caring for others and focusing on ourselves, something I describe as the "Relational Rectangle."

The Relational Rectangle

I was sitting in church one spring Sunday thinking about things in life that are mutually exclusive, when I should have been thinking about the sermon. It was at the time when my annual spring allergies arrive, making me sneeze from grass and birch tree pollen. I'm miserable for about eight weeks during spring, and even though I take medication for the problem, I still sneeze a great deal.

One day, as I was driving down the freeway, a monster of a sneeze erupted from my nose. I then noticed that at the height of the sneeze, my eyes involuntarily closed for a second. Not a good thing to happen while driving, even if it's only for a moment. That's when it hit me, sneezing and keeping my eyes open are mutually exclusive. I can't do both. So when driving on the freeway, I try really hard to suppress a sneeze coming on in order to keep my eyes open.

The first time I explained this to a group, my friend Roger got all animated and chimed in, "When I was in boot camp training in the Marine Corps, they told us if we were ever in a fox hole and had to keep really quiet near enemy lines, there was one technique we could use to suppress a sneeze. Rather than trying to not sneeze, try really hard to keep your eyes open, because when your eyes are open, you can't sneeze."

Caring for others is like this, too. You can't care well for people if you're focusing on yourself and all your needs. It's like a rectangle divided into two triangles.

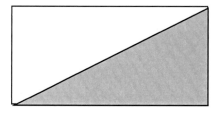

The top part of the rectangle, the white triangle, represents focusing our attention and energies on anything related to me and my concerns. It's all about me and what I'm thinking about and concerned with.

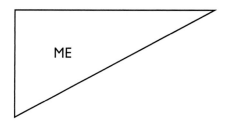

Right below this **ME** triangle, we have another triangle, a **YOU** triangle. This represents our attention and focus on another person. It's about thinking and concerning ourselves with the needs of someone else, and looking at life from another person's perspective.

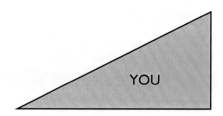

If we put both triangles together, we get a rectangle, which gets me dangerously close to the precipice of my knowledge of geometry. We have now created a Relational Rectangle.

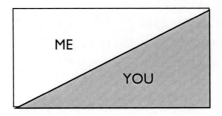

You can plot the state of any relationship by drawing a vertical line, anywhere from left to right, as you can see in the diagram below. In the small vertical white and gray rectangle on the left, within the larger horizontal rectangle, notice how much white (Me) there is compared to the gray (You). The white (Me) takes up most of the room in the newly created vertical rectangle, so there is little room for the gray (You).

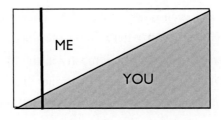

The Relational Rectangle depicts the mutually exclusive nature about caring for others. It illustrates that at any point in time, to the extent we are focused on our needs, wants, worries, and issues of life, we will have diminished capacity to attend to someone else. Our intentions may be pure and other-centered, but the more self-centered our behavior, the less wherewithal we have to care about someone else.

We can also draw a different vertical line on the right side of the larger rectangle, and there you will see how the gray **YOU** crowds out the white **ME** in this smaller vertical rectangle. When we set aside our needs and concerns for the moment, we increase our capacity to care for the needs of someone other than ourselves. Our relationships are like this vertical line, moving left to right, and right to left. The more we slide to the right of the relational rectangle, the more we're tuned into another person, and the less we're focused on ourselves.

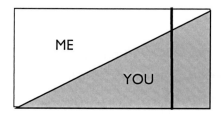

One can easily see this dynamic played out when people talk to one another. If I were to take a video recorder and record people having conversations with each other, it would be interesting to plot for each person in the conversation where along the diagonal line the vertical line would intersect. Who is living mostly in the **ME**, and who is living more in the **YOU** would be easy to determine. One important marker in analyzing this is to note the number of times the topic of conversation changes.

Conversations in which both parties are living in the **ME** are like a game of table tennis, where the topics go back and forth over the net, and nothing lingers to allow further deepening discussion. It's also like two race cars with engines revving at top rpms at the starting line. They're waiting for the checkered flag to drop so they can put the car in gear, press the pedal to the metal, and roar down the track to talk about themselves. People in these conversations are not listening; they're just waiting to talk.

Conversations with **YOU** people are very different. They are more like a game of golf, with two golfers sharing the same ball. They follow the ball around the course at a leisurely pace, taking turns picking up the train of thought wherever the ball lands on the course. This dichotomy of **ME** and **YOU** goes beyond conversations, though. It speaks to the heart of how we live our lives.

ME People

Those who live in the **ME** portion of the Relational Rectangle have certain characteristics. Most of us know someone who is a poster child for someone living a **ME** centered life. These are the people in our lives who seem to have "Life is All About Me" tattooed on their foreheads. They are people who can only see the world through their eyes, and who only care about things that directly affect them.

If it doesn't impact them, it doesn't matter. If you can't help me or advance my agenda in some way, then you don't matter. What only matters is **ME**.

ME people talk more than they listen. They don't listen well because they don't want to. If life is all about me, what possible benefit would there be to listen to you? The only value in listening to you is to prompt me to talk about **ME**. When you share your thoughts and experiences, it gives me an opportunity to talk far more about mine. I can use everything you say to relate to my own thoughts and experiences, which gives me the floor to talk about **ME**, a floor I will be most reluctant to give back to you.

C.S. Lewis describes this quite succinctly when he says, "Satan is the author of incessant autobiography."

As a **ME** person, I'm more interested in things and events than I am in people. Things and events are what feed me, as they give me a platform to talk about **ME**. Things and events don't require much of us. People do. It's easy for me to talk about cars, recipes, and computers. They are things, and often come with manuals to explain themselves and to tell us how to repair them when they break.

People aren't like things. We don't come with manuals, online or otherwise. Our families, co-workers, and neighbors are hard to figure out at times. It's much more comfortable to center our lives around things, even when those things break. When they break, we might be able to fix them ourselves or hire someone to do the repair. And if a thing is broken beyond repair, we can discard it and buy a new one. With people, not so much.

If my relationship with my spouse breaks, sure, I can get a divorce, but that's a lot more expensive than repairing the washing machine. If my relationship with my mother fractures, I can't get a new one. I'm stuck with the mother I have, not the mother I want. These important relationships have a way of affecting us in ways that broken things don't.

Even if my ex- is long gone and remarried, or my mother passed away ten years ago, these important relationships still affect me. The car that blew a transmission, or the water heater that rusted out, no longer have a hold on me when I discard them. Not so with people. Better to revolve my life around things than people—that's how a **ME** person goes through life.

The same is true with recreational events. We can live for our next vacation, next concert, next ballgame, next party. Events bring us pleasure and excitement that is out of the ordinary. They're a break in our routine. They require little of us except to sit back and enjoy, unless, of course, we're the one sponsoring the event, like Thanksgiving dinner for all our dysfunctional family members.

Some **ME** people build their lives around events. It's easy to occupy ourselves in preparing for events, and then enjoying the all-too-short afterglow following them. The more we fill our lives with events and things, the less room we have for people.

ME people usually don't initiate much with others. They're more reactors when it comes to relationships, unless it's to further something about them. *But if I have nothing to gain in initiating, what's the sense of being proactive?* Not much, according to ME people.

Other characteristics of ME people include:

- Difficulty in understanding the viewpoint of others
- More self-protected than YOU people
- Often see themselves as victims when things go badly
- Come with large egos
- Need to be right many times
- More competitive than most
- Have high expectations of others

Examples of ME people include small children, and most characters in TV sitcoms. Infants and toddlers I can handle; we all come out the womb self-centered. Adults in some TV shows are another matter. *The Office*, *Friends*, and *Seinfeld* are loaded with ME people—characters totally consumed with getting their needs met, even at the expense of other people.

YOU People

Those who live in the YOU in the relational rectangle are very different from ME people. They are more interested in people and ideas than things and events. Introverts and extroverts can both feel at home living in the YOU triangle. It's not how outgoing they are; it's how other-centered they are that makes the difference. **YOU** people generally are inquisitive about others, not to satisfy some curiosity need, but rather from a desire to know and understand others. While some relationships can be draining, **YOU** people, for the most part, find them enriching. People are a fascinating way to broaden our world, according to a **YOU** person.

Interesting conversations about ideas are sought after by **YOU** people. They gravitate toward others who think beyond the mundane here and now. They do this because **YOU** people have the capacity and interest in seeing life from someone else's perspective. This broadens one's world, and **YOU** people tend to live broad, other-centered lives.

A **YOU** person, in contrast to its **ME** counterpart, will often initiate and be proactive in relationships. They take a measure of control over what they want in relationships by extending themselves to others. **YOU** people tend to have more empathy and compassion than those in the **ME** triangle, for they have an easier time putting themselves in the place of someone else. They can see life from the perspective of someone else. **YOU** people tend to be more generous with their time than **ME** people.

Another interesting characteristic of **YOU** people is the grace and tolerance they extend to others. Their expectations of others are decidedly lower than **ME** people. I came across a study recently that concluded the people of Sweden are the happiest people on earth. Why? Because they have lower expectations of others than any other nation, according to this study. And here I thought it was their meatballs and shopping at IKEA.

Young mothers are great examples of **YOU** people. They wake in the middle of the night when they sense something wrong with the baby. They're so occupied with meeting the physical needs of their child they often don't think of their own needs. The first responders to the Twin Towers on 9/11 were certainly living in the **YOU** that day.

Debra, in *Everyone Loves Raymond*, shows glimpses of being a YOU person every so often. She challenges her husband occasionally, "You know, Ray, what you said to your brother Robert was not very kind. Don't you think he could be hurt by the thoughtless comment you made?" None of the other characters from that TV show, or most other sitcoms, would ever consider life from beyond their own ME portion of the Relational Rectangle.

* * * * *

I once spoke to a group of missionaries about the Relational Rectangle and the notion we can't relate well with others and care for them if we're living in the ME and focusing our energies on ourselves. They pushed back on this concept with comments like, "What about self-care? How can we care for others if we're not caring for ourselves?"

That particular group had a number of hurting people going through some great difficulties. I tried to make the point that there are times we need to live in the ME, time when we need to regroup and replenish our energies. It's perfectly appropriate when we need to reflect on our lives and where we've come from, and where we are going. Missionaries on home assignment especially need to re-charge their batteries and take in more than they give out. I get it, I really do.

But sometimes we play the self-care and self-love cards to justify our self-centeredness. We ignore the reality that many times caring for others and living in the YOU is the very thing we need to care for ourselves. You'd be hard pressed to find anything in the Bible supporting the notion that before we can care or love others, we have to do the same for ourselves.

Self-care and self-love are never prerequisites for caring for others. There are many verses in the Bible to support just the opposite, like Paul's first letter to the Corinthians, chapter 10 and verse 24, "Don't be concerned for your own good but for the good of others." I don't see how we can ignore that. Imagine if we all obeyed that for just thirty minutes a day. That's only two percent of a 24-hour day.

Maybe we could start a 2% church. We have 2% milk, where the 2% refers to the bad stuff, the fat. Why not a 2% church that focuses on the good stuff: caring for others? We could have a cow in our logo. I know it would play well in Wisconsin where I'm from. In time, the Church of the 2% could even become a denomination.

A focus on others to the exclusion of self is a wonderful, enriching form of self-care. Even during our worst days, when life is so difficult or painful for us, where it's so hard to think about anything but ourselves, taking even thirty minutes out of twenty-four hours to center our attention on others can be a great healing and energizing activity.

Living in the YOU and channeling our energies to concern ourselves with the needs of others brings out the best in us. It reflects the character of God, and helps us to become more the men and women God designed us all to be. It brings us out of ourselves and engages us in a world so much broader and richer than the narrow existence we sometimes create for ourselves.

Maybe it's just me, but I find myself quite boring at times. Thinking about the same old junk I've been thinking about for many years. Stuff about me. I'm yawning as I write this. How much more interesting it is to get out of myself and pay more attention to the people and world around me than the inner world of self.

We can't live in both worlds of ME and YOU at the same time. They are mutually exclusive, like wheelchairs and pogo sticks. That, by the way, is a retail store I'd love to open next to *Just Oak and More*. Imagine the diverse customer base who'd shop at *Wheelchairs and Pogo Sticks*. I'd love the challenge of cross-selling in a shop like that.

"Welcome to our store! We have a sale going on now. With each wheelchair purchase, we'll take thirty percent off on a new pogo stick."

I find myself feeling very comfortable living a **ME** life, because living a **YOU** life requires more of me from time to time than I want to give. What's required is so often a decision to set my needs aside for the moment for the benefit of another person.

A neighbor of mine ran into such a dilemma. I can so identify with him. We had a gathering at his home one night, and the other neighbors learned ahead of time that the night of our get-together was my birthday. Each of them brought a small birthday gift for me. My neighbor and friend, the host, didn't know about my birthday, so he had no gift. The situation greatly unnerved our host. I watched him talk to my wife Janet in their kitchen, frantically opening cabinet doors, looking for something to give me.

"Do you think John would like this bottle of wine?" he whispered to Janet.

"No, he doesn't drink wine; it gives him headaches," Janet replied.

"Uh, oh. Well, I'll give it to him anyway."

The "gift" was all about his living in the **ME**, though it was in the context of a **YOU** situation, giving someone a gift. Our dear friend, who lives in the **YOU** so much of his life, had a **ME** moment in which his prime concern was relieving his awkwardness in not having a gift when everyone else did. His actions were all about him, and had nothing to do with me. We are both so much alike in this regard.

I so identify with being concerned what people think about me to the extent it gets in the way of sound judgment. Like my friend, all of us slide up and down the diagonal line of the Relational Rectangle. One minute, we're completely focused on the needs of another person, two seconds later, we're consumed with our own needs and image.

Another example occurred one Easter Sunday several years ago. Janet's father had been admitted to a rehab facility within a nursing home following heart surgery. Janet's mom was living with us, and after we went to church that morning, we decided to pick up our seven-year-old twin grandsons and their three-year-old sister, who live two miles away to go and visit Janet's dad.

The journey did not start well. Loaded with Easter candy, they climbed into our mini-van arguing with each other and calling upon me to right the injustice each of them were experiencing at the hands of their siblings.

"Why can't I sit on that side, he ALWAYS gets to sit where HE wants."

"She touched me. Stop it."

"Grandpa, do something! Why do you always believe HIM and not ME?"

All on Easter Sunday. All to show once again you never have to teach children to look out for their own best interests. It comes as standard equipment, just like the car seats on which they were sitting. They all live in the ME.

Fortunately, the rehab facility was not far away, but the bickering continued all the way there and on into the entrance of the building once we arrived. Back and forth they were at each other until we found Janet's dad in the cafeteria. Once they entered the large room, though, everything changed.

It was quite startling. Around a dozen or so large circular tables sat two or three residents to a table. All in varying states of consciousness. Some asleep with chins on their chests. Some staring off into the distance with a comatose stare. Still others talking to no one in particular as drool dripped down their faces. This jaw-dropping scene silenced the kids like nothing else could.

They soon found Janet's dad off in the distance. Their eyes and his brightened as they ran over to his table. They always seemed to energize him. Grant reached into his bag of Easter candy and said, "Hi, Great-Grandpa, would you like a piece of my Easter candy?"

"Sure," he said. He was the most alert resident in the room. The other two grandkids offered more of their candy, which he was all too pleased to accept.

Grant then turned from his great-grandfather and slowly surveyed the rest of the room. And with no prompting from anyone, began approaching the other residents, asking them if they too would like a piece of his Easter candy. Some nodded their heads affirmingly, so Grant placed the candy in their hands. Others did not respond at all, but he placed a piece of candy on the table in front of them anyway. He continued distributing his candy to the other residents; then his brother and sister followed his lead and started to do the same thing.

After all the residents had been approached, the three grandkids began offering their candy to any of the staff who happened to be in the room. Once they completed this, they started walking down the hall and went into resident rooms with open doors. (We quickly stopped that.)

Here they were, one minute totally consumed with their own selfish needs, firmly entrenched in the ME, then seconds later, freely giving away their candy they so enjoyed. The speed at which they moved from ME to YOU was quite remarkable.

We can all move from ME to YOU just as quickly. When we want to. The reverse also is true, for we can move from YOU to ME as rapidly and dramatically.

It happened to me the day Grant came home from the hospital.

* * * * *

As mentioned in an earlier chapter, our grandson Grant and his twin brother George were born quite prematurely. As a result, they both spent many weeks in the hospital after their births. First George came home, then his brother two weeks later. What a joyous occasion it was when Grant came home to be with his womb mate and the rest of his family. I remember driving with Janet over to our son's condo to see the boys for the first time in their new home. I was flooded with joy over their survival and how God had spared their lives. I was so filled with gratitude, so filled with happiness. So filled with every-thing that is good. Life could not have been any better for me than it was the morning we drove to Michael and Hope's home to see the boys.

It all changed in an instant when we drove into their condo complex and saw Hope's parents' car parked in front of their home.

"What are THEY doing here?" I steamed inside. "How come THEY'RE here?"

I could feel my blood pressure rising. This was to be our moment. Our time. And here THEY were raining on our parade. *This can't be. This is supposed to be about ME enjoying this wonderful moment. I don't want to share this time. It's mine!* I slipped so quickly from living in the YOU and thinking about God saving the boys, but within a nano-second, all I could think about was ME. It happened so quickly.

I completely ignored Hope's parents and what everything meant to them. THEY are wonderful people and love our son and grandkids just as much as we do, but in this ugly moment of mine when we pulled up to the condo, all I could think about was feeling robbed. I felt like a victim. Please don't share this with anyone, because it's quite embar-rassing.

People who live in the ME often feel like victims as I did, but when the voice of reason, through the Holy Spirit, got through to me, guilt over my selfishness brought me back to reality. Guilt can be a good thing at times.

Relating well with others and caring about them is mutually exclusive with a preoccupation with our needs and desires, just as *Just Oak and More* and *Wheelchairs and Pogo Sticks* are mutually exclu-sive. We think we can have it all, but we can't. It's part of living in our fallen world east of Eden. It's like shopping at a strip mall with stores like *Just Oak and More* and *Wheelchairs and Pogo Sticks*. We can also shop at adjacent shops, like the BR & WW boutique (a joint venture between Baskin Robbins Ice Cream and Weight Watchers).

But at the end of the strip of stores and offices, I can imagine a storefront called *YOU and ME*. It would be a counseling clinic where therapists repeatedly drive home the point that in spite of what the magazines say, you can't have it all. You can't even have it both ways. You have to make a choice. You have to decide between being a **YOU** or a **ME** person.

The therapists at *YOU and ME* would not be licensed counselors; they wouldn't delve into your past to discover how you were toilet trained, nor would they interpret what you see in the ink blots of a Rorschach test. They would just listen to you, and help you decide what kind of person you want to be. If you want to be a **ME** person, they would help you recognize this in yourself, and explain the consequences of living that kind of life. No judgment at all about your choice would be offered by them. None at all. Once you understood your choice, you'd be free to leave.

However, if you decided you wanted to be a **YOU** person, you'd be ushered down a hallway to the **YOU** suite where you would meet your **YOU** therapist.

"Hello, my name is Angela, I will be helping you today, and in the days to come, to become the **YOU** person you want to be. I should let you know that my role is to teach you just one thing, the most important thing to become more of a **YOU** person."

"Just one thing? Is that all it takes to be a **YOU** person?"

"Yes, just one thing," Angela replies.

This sounds like it's going to be easy. Learning just one thing—I can do this.

"It could very well be the hardest thing you've ever done in your life," Angela responds.

"Really? Well, how long will it take to learn this one thing?"

"Many years."

Huh? Many years? "Is this like algebra or statistics? That's the only thing I can think of that would take many years for me to learn. I'm a pretty bright person; I can program my DVR. But math always does me in."

"Math and programming a DVR are all about the head. What I'm going to teach you is all about your heart," Angela replies.

"Well, what is it then? What's the one thing you're going to teach me that will turn me into a YOU person?"

"Sometimes, when I answer this question, people are not ready to hear what I have to say. Sometimes they don't believe me, that it could only be one thing," Angela replies.

"C'mon, Angela. That's your name, right?"

"Yes."

"Tell me then, what is the one thing you're going to teach me to become more of a YOU person?

"OK. Here it is. I'm going to teach you how to listen," Angela concludes.

Listen?

Chapter 18

Thank You for Asking

The beauty of listening is that, those who are listened to start feeling
accepted, start taking their words more seriously
and start discovering their own true selves.
—Henri Nouwen

What an odd expression, *thank you for asking*. It's usually said in response to someone who remembers some detail about our life and is now following up with a question about that detail. *Thank you for asking* strikes me as odd in that why should we ever have to thank someone for being a good listener and inquiring about our life? It's odd because it happens all too rarely, people listening to us and remembering what we told them when we saw them last. I guess it's more sad than it is odd that we don't listen well to each other.

There's something quite encouraging and affirming when someone listens to us, and then later remembers what we said. Among other things, listening to another gives the other person a voice. Like many, I did not have a voice growing up. There was so much going on inside of me that no one knew about.

One of the first people who ever listened to me was Janet, whom I met as freshmen in high school and later married. One of the things that attracted me to her was how she wanted to get to know me by asking questions. She asked about my home life, which was so different from her own. As I grew to trust her, I would tell her more and more.

Janet asked questions, like, "How come your parents won't let you get a driver's license?" "What do your parents yell and hit you for?" "Why do you work so many hours at your after-school job?"

One question she never asked me was "Why doesn't the basketball coach put you in the game more often?"

I think she knew—I just wasn't very good. I was barely good enough to make the team my senior year in high school. I sat at the end of the bench with my friend, "Harry the Cat" Brill. He didn't get to play much either. We called him "Harry the Cat" because he ran up and down the court like a cat. I loved watching him in practice. He had very long legs and it always looked like he was running in slow motion, but he wasn't. He was just graceful.

We had a good team our senior year and were conference champions. Harry the Cat and I got into games when we were beating the other team by a large margin. The last home game of the year was against the worst team in the conference, so our coach put Harry the Cat and me into the game as starters. We played the whole first quarter, and then again at the end of the last quarter during mop-up time. On the one hand, it felt great to start for the first time all season, but on the other hand, I felt patronized.

I didn't know what patronized meant then, but I felt it though I had no words to express it. But Janet knew how I felt and that helped. She could tell. She listened to how I was feeling. Listening well is not limited to words. We listen well when we pick up on other signals. Watery eyes. A twitching lower lip. A downcast glance. A smile that just won't quit. Shoulders leaning forward eager to engage. Sometimes these tell us more than words. Listening well is just as much about our eyes as it is about our ears. Janet was good at that. Still is.

The following Monday after our last regular season game, I walked into our locker room to suit up for practice for the start of post-season tournament play. As I headed to my locker, our coach called Harry the Cat and me into his office.

"Boys, as you know the state basketball tournament starts with sectional games this Friday. There are two guys on the JV team I want to bring up to varsity to give them playing time in preparation for next year. But that means I have to cut two other guys to make room for them. Unfortunately, I'm going to have cut both of you. I'll need you to clean out your lockers now and turn in your practice jerseys. I want you to know, though, you're both welcome to ride on the team bus to wherever we're playing in the tournament."

He didn't know he was delivering this news to me on my 18th birthday.

I never went to another game.

When I told Janet I had been cut from the team, she just listened. She couldn't fix it, and she didn't try. But Janet could see how I felt because she imagined how it would feel if she were on a high school basketball team and had just been cut from the team to make room for a sophomore on the tournament roster.

A lot of listening is trying to imagine what life is like for another person. Janet did that well and her listening to me in those days was a powerful tool that helped me get through high school.

* * * * *

I don't think Ken Burns will be contacting me anytime soon to produce a PBS documentary about my life, or how we can all care for each other better. But if he did, I would include my national media exposure on National Public Radio in March 2005. I was interviewed about an event that occurred late one cold, sunny Saturday afternoon at a Sheraton Hotel three miles from our home.

A gunman stormed into a large meeting room of the hotel and opened fire with his rifle on a group of fifty to sixty people gathered together for an event, killing seven people, and then himself.

The nature of the event? A church service.

Yes, a church service. The killer was a member of this small religious sect, not an outsider. Witnesses said he came to the service, but left near the beginning. He went back home and returned with weapons that he turned on his pastor and fellow church members.

Several days after the shooting, I drove past the hotel on the way to my office and saw makeshift crosses at one of the side entrances. Why had this horror taken place in a church service, of all places, is a question I couldn't shake all morning. On my lunch hour, I drove back to the scene to look at the crosses. Several other people were already there looking at each cross, along with an inconspicuous reporter from NPR. He came up to me and asked me why I was there.

"On my way to work this morning, I saw the crosses, and I guess I'm trying to process this terrible event and what caused it. You wouldn't expect something like this to happen in a church service."

That's all I said. What I didn't say was, "*What could have possessed a member of this small church body to become so angry as to take the life of his pastor and six other church members? What could have been so terrible that he took this awful action? You wouldn't think this would happen within a church congregation. Aren't churches supposed to be places where people care for one another, not kill each other?*"

The event raised questions for me about church in general and the role it plays in people caring for one another. I suppose one could explain the tragedy with talk of psychological disorders, demon possession, or just plain evil. It could very well be all of these things. I don't know. But it still seems to me the church in general could do a better job of caring for its own by creating an environment that encourages all of us to listen to each other better.

Listening not just about the news, the kids, or all the activities of life. It's more than that. It's about listening to each other's hearts, and to our hopes and dreams, the things we worry about, the things we regret.

I once heard a pastor of a church of about 1,000 say this about listening: "I would pay good money to find someone who would just sit among our people and listen to them. Many people have no one to listen to them." The pastor was on to something. Many of us live lonely, depressed lives because we have no one to listen to us. Sure, there are people we can talk to and talk with, but are they really listening? What looks like listening is often people waiting to talk. Usually about themselves.

I grew up in the Roman Catholic Church and one of the things I liked about my early church days was the sacrament of confession. People would line up to go into a the confessional booth to confess their sins to a priest. He sat in the middle on a wooden bench, flanked by a chamber on either side where the confessing person would kneel. No one could see the priest and he couldn't see you. But you could hear each other when he slid open a small door that barely covered a black screen about a foot square. We still couldn't see each other, but with this door open, we could hear one another. The priest was someone who would listen, but he only listened to the bad stuff we did. He never got to hear the good stuff. It wasn't in his training manual. He never got to hear things like:

Father, I just got a new job.

Father, my husband and I just found out I'm pregnant with our first child. I'm so happy.

I have a few things to confess, Father, but first I want to tell you I got a promotion and raise at work.

Priests don't get to hear about the joys of life in the confessional.

I wonder if the shooter who killed his pastor and six others had anyone to listen to him. I suspect not. The church for him appeared to be a source of pain, not a cure for it. I think of the contrast between my own church and the shooter's church experience. I think of all the people in our church who cared for our friend Jill when she took in four foster kids, and wonder if there was anyone in the killer's congregation who ever reached out to him. Maybe there was and we don't know it.

That tragic event made me wonder if I am falling down on the job of listening to others in my church. Am I noticing people enough and picking up on non-verbal cues? Or am I too self-absorbed with my own struggles to take notice of other struggling people?

Just the other day, thirteen-year-old grandson George looked at Janet and said, "Grandma, you look a little stressed today."

She was, which led to an interesting discussion between grandson and grandmother about stress. A conversation started by a young teenager thinking about someone other than himself, who listened with his eyes, and then made an observation. He already is a good listener, and will only get better in time. Becoming a good listener is something learned and practiced.

Sometimes the church makes it hard for us to be heard, especially for those of us who have been marginalized in other areas of our life. The church is really strong in talking, as in sermons. The preacher gives a sermon and the people in the pew listen to it. We sorely need good preaching in the church, and we need to hear well what the priest or minister is saying. After all, when they bring their A-game to the pulpit, we are hearing what God has for us through them.

But most churches don't function so well as organizations when it comes to listening. Two churches I've attended at one time or another solicited feedback from the congregation in the form of letter or notes to be put in a suggestion box. In each case, the congregation was put on notice with "Please sign your name to whatever you give us. No anonymous suggestions or complaints will be considered. Anything that comes in without a name is thrown away unread."

Having served on several church boards, I understand why it's helpful to know who is making comments and suggestions. They're easier to deal with. And while it's true some people may hide behind their anonymity to unleash criticisms, there are also some very good reasons why a congregant may want to remain anonymous.

Some people wish to remain anonymous because they don't want to be perceived as complainers. Some people wish to remain anonymous because they are private by nature and do not want to draw attention to themselves. Some prefer anonymity because they want their suggestion to be judged on its merits, and not on who is presenting it. Others want to remain anonymous because they have a legitimate observation, but they don't want any action taken. Still others wish to remain unknown because, while they have a suggestion, they do not want to be drawn into a discussion about it. And some people choose anonymity because they've come out of church backgrounds where they've had bad experiences with church leaders and don't trust them.

Because someone prefers to remain anonymous should not be reason alone to discount what a person has to say. To disregard any anonymous suggestion is to suppress communication from the congregation, not enhance it. It automatically disqualifies those who want anonymity from having a voice in the life of the church.

It also speaks to a low view of people, assuming one's desire to remain nameless has less than a virtuous motive behind it. *We will not respond to any suggestions that are anonymous* comes across as the leadership wanting to insulate itself from criticism, which dampens any good will achieved by asking for input in the first place.

Instead of disqualifying the anonymous, I'm for giving people the benefit of the doubt and respecting their privacy. Trust that in most cases, their reasons for wanting anonymity are as I've described. Judge

the comments or suggestions on their merits. Whether they're anonymous or attributed to an individual shouldn't matter. Good suggestions
and bad suggestions come from both places. Focus on the message, not
the messenger.

Individuals within a church, or any group for that matter, tend to do
a better job of listening than the institution itself. Listening doesn't cure
all the world's ills, but it does give people a voice. Some of us are
verbal processors and we need someone to talk to, to listen. When we
talk to someone who is truly listening, it helps us clarify what we're
thinking and feeling. From there, we can often figure out on our own
how to move on with life.

It's interesting how politicians will often hold what they call
"Listening Sessions" in their home districts. They meet for an hour or
two at a town hall to find out what's on the voters' minds. I have never
been to one, but my guess is a lot of complaining goes on. "How come
our taxes are so high? Why can't you get this done? When are you
going to get that done?" If I were a politician, I don't think I'd look
forward to these. You need to have a thick skin to be a politician.
People in ministry also need to have thick skins.

Imagine what it would be like if churches, mission agencies, and
other organizations held listening sessions from time to time like
politicians do. Imagine inviting people to share what they're thinking
and wanting from the organizations they belong to? I suspect there
would be a fair amount of asking for this or that, and it might get testy
at times. But it would give people a voice, make them feel heard, and
perhaps even generate a positive idea or two that could benefit the
organization. Too often, though, we don't want to listen to people
because we're afraid of what they might say, and what they might
expect of us.

* * * * *

Listening well can change a life. It happened to me in high school one day at the beginning of my senior year in a routine obligatory appointment with my guidance counselor, a person I had never spoken to before. Shirley Roller called me into her office, as she and the other guidance counselors did with all seniors, and asked me what my plans were for next year after I graduated. I told her I was planning to live at home and commute to a college in town.

"Is that what you want to do, go to college as a commuter student?"

"Well, not really. I'd like to leave home and go away to a college where I could live in a dorm. But I don't have enough money to do that."

"What about applying for financial aid so you could?"

"I checked into that and found that my parents would have to fill out a confidential statement about their finances. When I asked them to do this, my dad said he wouldn't. He said it was nobody's business how much money he made. He wondered why I would want to go to college in the first place, as he thought it would be a waste of money. He didn't think I was smart enough to go."

"Your grades and test scores indicate you're smart enough," she said.

"Yeah, I'm going to go to college anyway, but here in town because that's all I can afford."

"How are you going to pay for college?"

"Since tenth grade, I've been working at a restaurant, putting in long hours, except during basketball season, when I only work Saturdays and Sundays. I've been saving the money for college. I think I'll have enough to go to school here in town."

After a long pause, Mrs. Roller asked me another really important question, "What if I could get financial aid for you without your parents having to fill out the parents' confidential statement? Would you want to go away to college then?"

"Can you really do that? Really? If you could, sure. I'd love to go away to school."

"If you could go away to college, where would you like to go?"

When I dreamed about going away to college, Eau Claire kept coming up. Only a handful of my classmates were planning to attend this Wisconsin state university, and the 250 miles from home seemed like the other side of the moon, just the perfect distance from home. There was no other reason to go there. I didn't know anything about the school, other than it was pretty much like all the other state universities. It was the distance and the sound of the name, Eau Claire, French for "clear water," that drew me. How profound. How reasoned, logical, and measured. How pathetic.

"I'd love to go to Eau Claire. Can you really get financial aid for me without my dad filling out that form?"

"I will try, but there are no guarantees. There is some financial aid for students in your situation, so I will make some phone calls and see what I can do. I can't promise you anything. But I'll get back to you."

"Wow. Thank you."

I sat stunned.

Could it be possible? How could she do that for me? Did she know how messed up my home life was? Had someone told her? How would she know that my leaving home to go away to college would be like letting someone out of prison?

I should have said, "Thanks for asking," but the phrase hadn't been invented yet.

Shirley Roller gave me the gift of hope. Hope that maybe I could afford to leave home after all, and no longer have to cross out each passing day on the calendar with a big black X like Jimmy Cagney sitting in a cell at Sing Sing. What a wonderful thing it is to give people hope. She gave me hope by listening.

Mrs. Roller was one of those people God placed in my life at just the right time who asked just the right question, *Is that what you really want to do?* That simple question changed my life. If it wouldn't have been for her asking that question, I don't know where I'd be today. What a great question, *Is that what you want to do?* It's one of those questions that very innocently, yet powerfully, invites a person to reflect on decisions he or she is facing. It gives voice to choice.

So many times in life, we think we have no choice when in reality, we have more choices than we think. There are times when the consequences of choices are not appealing, but we have choices nevertheless. Not all the time, of course. But we don't have to live as victims, thinking there's nothing we can do.

Within a few weeks of our first encounter, Shirley Roller called me back to her office to tell me she contacted the financial aid office at what is now the University of Wisconsin—Eau Claire. She was happy to report they were offering me a financial aid package of grants, loans, and work-study employment, all without my parents having to sign anything. I couldn't believe it then, and I can't believe it now. What a great undeserved blessing that came my way, all because someone cared enough to ask two insightful, probing questions.

I went on to graduate from Eau Claire, because Shirley Roller listened to me. And she listened to more than my words. Maybe it was my countenance. Maybe it was my dejection and resignation that I was going to have to live at home for a few more years that prompted her to ask *is that what you really want to do.* It wasn't my words, that's for sure, for I had never talked about my home life with any adult. Whatever it was, she listened.

If Mrs. Roller hadn't listened, and I had never gone to Eau Claire, I can't imagine how my life would have turned out. It was at Eau Claire I discovered my dad was wrong and that I did have what it takes to make it in life. It was at Eau Claire where my relationship with Janet grew to the point we got married. It was at Eau Claire where I became a father. It was at Eau Claire I grew to love history and writing. It was at Eau Claire I found Jesus.

I don't think much anymore about what a dark, damp cave my high school years were, but when I do, I can snap out of it pretty easily when I think about Shirley Roller and how God used her to care for me. She entered my cave and showed me how to get out, to move toward the faint light at the cave's opening. She did it by listening.

So many wonderful things happen when we listen.

On several occasions years later, I tried tracking down Mrs. Roller to thank her, but I never did locate her. The last I heard, she left her position at our high school and moved to Rockford, Illinois. I wish I would have tried finding her when I graduated from college, but by that time, I was too absorbed in myself and my teaching career to think about the important people in my life who helped me get to where I was and wanted to be. The older I get, the more I reflect on the people I am thankful for.

The two questions Mrs. Roller asked me: *is that what you really want to do,* and *what if I could get financial aid for you...would you want to go away to college then* were pivotal in my life. They were both a means of unexpected caring from an unlikely source—a guidance counselor. She easily could have nodded in agreement when I told her I planned to attend college locally so she could move on to her next appointment. It's what most people would have done. Instead, she softly and subtly challenged me to look at what I wanted from life.

Good questions do that. They bring out the best in us when they cause us to reflect. Shirley Roller pushed the envelope a bit with her questions, which can be risky at times. We don't ask nearly enough questions of each other, in part because we're unwilling to take the risk of hearing how the other person might respond. The risk is often that perhaps more will be required of me, and I don't know if I want that in my life right now.

Asking questions brings out the best in not only the listener, but also the question-asker. Asking meaningful questions of others broadens our world and enhances our relationships.

Our grandsons George and Grant have always been great questioners. The first time I noticed their talent was when I started taking them to a barber when they were just toddlers. They were uncomfortable with getting haircuts at first (it made them itch), but as they got used to it and got to feel more comfortable with the barber, they began asking him questions, like how he got the stuffed deer head he mounted on the wall. Or the time they asked him, "Say, would you like to come to our house for dinner tonight?"

They both still ask me about how my day is going when I see them. Recently, I've been taking Grant to a math tutor. When I pick him up and ask him what he learned, he'll start by describing where in town his tutor lives, the tutor's favorite car, his day job, and what he likes to do in his free time.

"Grant, are you asking those questions to avoid getting help with your math?"

"No, not all," he responds. "People are really interesting and I like getting to know people."

Nowadays, when we're together, he'll ask me questions out of the blue like, "If you were attacked by a giant grizzly bear, what would you rather use to defend yourself—a spork, a very sharp knife, or a grenade launcher?" We then talk about the advantages of each, come up with a fourth alternative (like how about a sternly written note), and end up laughing about the silliness of it all. But these questions are his way of bonding with me. Questions can do that. They can draw us closer to each other.

* * * * *

Another person who listened to me, without ever asking me any questions, was my twelfth-grade English teacher, Phyllis Baumert. A former nun, she was tall, wore glasses, and had an elegance about her. When I talked or wrote about her, I referred to her as "The Lady." Because she was, in the best sense of the word. She didn't seem to mind. I could never picture her in a nun's habit. I always wondered why she left whatever order of nuns she belonged to. She never talked about it, and I wish I would have asked her. I think she would have told me.

We never talked to each other except in class discussions. Never outside of class. I lost out by not asking her questions about her life. But we did communicate through a journal I wrote. Everyone kept one as part of a class assignment. We were to write for two months. I wrote about all the things I was feeling, and things I was observing. It was a combination of *Catcher in the Rye* and a male version of *The Diary of Anne Frank.*

At the end of the two months, Miss Baumert collected the journals, and several weeks later, returned them to us. I looked through mine searching for my grade and her comments in red ink in the margins. I couldn't find any at first. It wasn't until the end of the journal that I found a note she had written on a page ripped out of a stenographer's notebook. In black ink in her always elegant hand, she wrote,

> *Here's a comment you may baste in or not—and that is a concession, in full consideration of the huge possibility of this [journal] being snatched from your very ownership and being published—posthumously though it may be.*
>
> *This is a fine journal—as good as any as I've ever read. You are painfully perceptive; very original and very crea-tive—and almost too full of insights for one your age to gracefully bear. I wish you were more confident of your*

powers of vision, personality, individual masculinity, and creativity. That way, you'd have less to prove. You should at least consider a career involving writing because it appears you have talent & insight & subtle humor.

I really enjoyed this journal, John. And I know you will find answers—but I hope not too soon—and I hope they don't come in the specific form of "answers."

A+ The Lady!

I lived on her note for months. Her listening to me through the words I wrote in my journal, and then her comments, were a soothing balm to my aching heart. Her remarks in my journal helped me realize I wasn't crazy. Listening well to another can give a person hope, as The Lady did for me. I did find answers, and they did not come quickly, as the Lady hoped they wouldn't—and they certainly didn't come in the specific form of answers. Her caring and sensitive wisdom still touches me forty-eight years later.

Little did either of us know that four years after she wrote the note, I would become an English teacher myself. And several years after that, I started giving my students the same assignment she had given me— write about what you are thinking, feeling, and observing. It was a 1970s version of a blog or Facebook post. And like Miss Baumert, I read each one of them carefully with my eyes and with my heart. Following her example, I looked and listened for ways to encourage and give hope to adolescents as messed up as I was back then. Her caring for me modeled how I could care for others. I wanted to be just like her.

Several years ago, I tried to locate her through Google. I found a funeral notice for a Phyllis Baumert in a small town in Nebraska. I hope that isn't her. I wanted to contact her and thank her for the impact she continues to have on my life. Maybe it's too late. I should have done it years ago.

I don't thank people who've impacted me at key moments in my life nearly as much as I should. It would benefit me more than them. I'd like to thank Phyllis Baumert for sharing a vision she had for what I could be. She said I could become a writer. Maybe someday, if she hasn't died yet, I'll write a book and give her a copy. It might encourage her to know she made a difference in the way she cared for me.

Listening well tends to do that.

Epilogue

hile Nobel laureate and Pulitzer Prize-winning author John Steinbeck was writing one of his most well-known novels, *East of Eden*, he wrote to his literary agent, Elizabeth Otis, "Never has a book so intrigued me. I only hope other people enjoy reading it as much as I enjoy writing it." Besides sharing the same birthday with Steinbeck, I also share his same feeling about this book, *THEM—The Richer Life Found in Caring for Others*.

I too hope people enjoy reading it as much as I enjoyed writing it. Not because I enjoyed retelling some of my story. Not at all. I've heard it before; I don't need to again. What intrigues me is how the stories of caring for others I've shared intersect with the larger story of God caring for all of humanity. Whether we're the caregiver or the care-receiver, when we connect all the dots, they take us back to God using people to orchestrate His care, concern, and compassion for His children, whom He loves beyond measure.

Unfortunately, we sometimes get in the way of God's care. Our pride, anger, and fractured relationships cause us to live narrow, self-contained lives. So does mishandling our fears, our self-centeredness, and letting our past define our present. We are a sorry lot left to our own devices. Fortunately, we have resources available to us from God, who wants to bring out the best in us, so we in turn can bring out the best in others.

Forgiveness and reconciliation, when we want it, result in God's releasing His power within us to give people grace, see life from another's perspective, and restore broken relationships. When we realize what God thinks of us is all that matters, the criticism of others no longer grips us, freeing us to be used for purposes larger than ourselves. Our lives expand greatly when we defer to others and live in humility, which makes God smile. So does getting in the boat with people going through great difficulty. God smiles even more when we join others in community in caring for people in need.

How we care for others and honor one another is limited only by our will, our want-to. We were made for caring relationships. If we look hard enough, and listen to God, we'll learn from all the stories playing out around us. We don't need a how-to book. God will show us Himself how we can live a much deeper, satisfying, and richer life by caring for others.

Additional Resources

For a free study guide to accompany this book for use in small groups, book clubs, or individual reflection, please visit John's blog, johncertalic.com, and click on "Free Study Guide for *THEM*." You can also follow his blog posts for all things related to caring for others.

Acknowledgments

I owe a debt of gratitude to my wife Janet, who gave me my first writing job back in high school when she was editor of our school newspaper. The feature column she asked me to write, *Off the Beaten Path*, introduced me to the satisfaction found in writing for an audience. She continues to be my best editor fifty years later, and was the one who spurred me on for several years to write this book. It never would have been written without her support and encouragement.

To my children, their spouses, and our grandchildren, whose stories are inextricably woven into mine, and which would be so much duller and unfulfilling if it were not for them. Thank you for putting up with me when I am at my worst. And to grandsons Grant and George, who frequently ask how much their royalties will be for using stories of them in the book, "The check is in the mail."

The present and former board members of Caring for Others, all of whom have been behind the writing of this book, are wonderful partners in ministry. To Judy Zwitter, Dr. Kathy Phelan, Dan Bunch, Mary Perso, Ed Larsen, and Michael Certalic, thank you for believing in the value of this project. One former board member in particular, Pastor Mike Frans, spurred me on especially in the beginning. Our occasional breakfasts together, even after he was off the board, were always seasoned with his genuine interest in how the book was coming along and his urging to not give up. Thank you, Mike, for all your encouragement.

To Karla Wyse, who read the beginning chapters of an early draft and offered a perspective more discerning than my own, thank you for getting me back on track with what was important, and encouraging me to delete what got in the way. You helped set the course for the book, for which I am grateful.

The encouragement of those who read advance reader copies of *THEM* has been more than I could have imagined. I so appreciate their taking time out of their busy schedules to read and comment on the content of the book. Many thanks to Stuart Briscoe, Dr. John Powell, Ruth Van Reken, Susan G., Jason and Kellie Knapp, Bill Schuit, Suzanne K., Devri Wickwire, Dr. Roni Pruitt, Pastor Bill Oliverio, Kathy McCready, Pastor Mike Frans, Gregg Hanchett, Dr. Jennifer Parsa, Eric G., and Pastor Rick Ribble.

Kira Henschel, of HenschelHAUS Publishing, who graciously and patiently educated me in the inner workings of the book publishing industry, thank you. You have taught me much, and have been a joy to work with. I will be forever in your debt for introducing me to the eleven pages in the *Chicago Manual of Style* devoted to the joys of using the hyphen properly. It has been an over-the-top-never-to-be-forgotten learning experience.

Finally, to the many missionaries we have been privileged to serve. Your stories continue to inspire me to draw closer to God as I've watched you do the same under conditions far more challenging than I face. My life is much fuller and richer because of all you have shared with Janet and me. Thank you for the privilege of allowing us to enter into your stories to see God at work for His glory and your good.

About the Author

John Certalic is the executive director of Caring for Others, a missionary care ministry whose purpose is to strengthen and encourage missionaries, and those who send them. Together with his wife Janet and volunteer colleagues, John and Caring for Others have ministered to over 1,000 missionaries from 62 different mission agencies, serving in 85 countries around the world.

John has an MS in counseling and lives with his wife Janet in New Berlin, Wisconsin—the only state in the Union with "sin" in its name. They have two grown children and four grandchildren.

Contact Information

For speaking, conference presentations, and missionary care needs, John can be reached here:

Blog: johncertalic.com
Website: www.caringforothers.org
Facebook: facebook.com/caringforothers
Twitter: twitter.com/johncertalic